For Bob Buetz—
To Our Perspicacious Colleague
Best Wishes

Jay Levy

David Levy

2/21/85

Profits and the Future of American Society

# PROFITS
# AND THE FUTURE
# OF AMERICAN
# SOCIETY

S JAY LEVY
AND
DAVID A. LEVY

*Illustrations by Edward P. O'Dell*

1817

HARPER & ROW, PUBLISHERS, New York
*Cambridge, Philadelphia, San Francisco, London,*
*Mexico City, São Paulo, Sydney*

FIRST EDITION

*Designer: Sidney Feinberg*

---

Library of Congress Cataloging in Publication Data

Levy, S Jay.
   Profits and the future of American society.
   Includes index.
   1. Profit—United States.    I. Levy, David A.
II. Title.
HC110.P7L48 1983     338.5'16'0973     81–47663
ISBN 0–06–014943–4                 AACR2

---

83 84 85 86 87 10 9 8 7 6 5 4 3 2 1

For Jerome Levy, 1882–1967,
who continues to illuminate the future

# Contents

# Acknowledgments

A gratifying aspect of writing this book was the enthusiasm and interest that the project evoked from friends and family. Their support and many hours of help enabled us to do a better job than would otherwise have been possible.

Leon Levy has played a special role. His long-standing interest, encouragement, and counsel helped us to conceive the book and shape its contents.

We are grateful for the comments of Eric Brus, Walter Mills, and Robert Samuelson, professional writers with different specialties, who generously gave a great many hours to help us improve our presentation. Our thanks also to Paul Argenti, who assisted with the editing of our 1980 monograph, *The Inevitable Inflation of the 1980s,* parts of which were adapted for this volume. Edward O'Dell, our artist, quickly understood the economic principles we were writing about and conceived how illustrations would help to explain them. Ann Levy's advice facilitated the conception and creation of the graphics.

Our good fortune also brought help from Professor Sidney Robbins and Peter L. Bernstein, two widely known economists who have written many admirable books. They aided us greatly by sharing their valuable experiences as authors and by raising cogent questions about our economic concepts.

Our staff at Industry Forecast was invaluable. We are especially indebted to Virginia Mills, who gave up weekends to work with us on the manuscript, drafted the charts, and generally shepherded the project. Elaine Berlind, who has a penchant for getting the right word and the right punctuation in place, was a continuing aid to us. Elaine Haimes rescued us from several emergencies, and Viviana Yamashita, a newcomer to our organization, arrived in time to help us complete the manuscript.

We are grateful to our editors at Harper & Row for their enthusiasm, sound judgments, and efforts on behalf of this book: Nancy Crawford, Robbin Reynolds, Hugh Van Dusen, and Janet Goldstein. We also thank Elizabeth Bartelme for her extensive and detailed editorial comments and our excellent copy editors, Brenda Goldberg and Diane Perez.

Writers, we have discovered, keep strange hours, eat at odd times, and even disappear for long periods. We are deeply grateful to our wives, Barbara Levy and Judith Butler Levy, for accommodating us in every conceivable way, and to Joshua Levy for his cheerful support. All three assisted us by offering unique insights from the vantage points of readers. Judi also undertook a substantial share of our research.

# Genesis

"If you were unemployed and were willing to work and able to work and could find no work, what would you do?"

The question was directed to William Howard Taft, candidate for the presidency.

"God knows," Taft replied. "I don't."

The year was 1908, and the future president had just completed a campaign speech at Cooper Union in New York City. Since the United States was in the midst of a recession—a "panic," as it was then called—the question from the audience was apt. The exchange was duly recorded by the local press.

The next morning, Jerome Levy, 26-year-old head of a small wholesale business, read about the incident in his newspaper. The young merchant, an erstwhile student of physics, mulled over Taft's candid admission and the problem of the unemployed.

"Taft was an able man," he later wrote. "I believed he was acquainted with the best books on economics and that he did not know the answer because it was not between their covers."

That morning, Jerome Levy became an economist. He believed that a man who is willing and able to work should have the opportunity to work.

I employ people, thought Jerome. I do so because I expect to make a profit. I spend $100 paying wages, buying merchandise, and so forth because I expect to get $110 back. I know how $100 of that $110 gets into circulation. I put it there. But *where does that other $10 come from?*

Where *do* profits come from? Jerome Levy zealously set out to answer this question. Because business hours in those days were eight to six, six days a week, he had to devote most of his spare time to this quest. By 1914, he had traced down the sources of profits and, in the process, acquired a view of capitalism that was more revealing than anyone else's. Seven decades later, we believe it still is.

Jerome found that his knowledge of profits enabled him to clearly understand and confidently anticipate economic events. Early in 1929, he decided to liquidate his business and his holdings in the stock market. He devoted the rest of his life to studying the economy and trying to interest others in his research.

However, a salesman and publicist he was not. His efforts to promote his discoveries were vigorous but not effective. Jerome would direct a discourse on the economic system at anyone who happened to be sitting next to him on a park bench or a bus. He frequently wrote letters outlining economic programs to prime ministers, treasury ministers, and other high officials the world over. Although these proposals had no perceivable effect, their author's enthusiasm was undiminished.

In 1949 Jerome and his two sons, Leon and Jay, decided that people would take notice of a practical demonstration of economic knowledge. Because of his education in physics, Jerome knew that one way to test a theory is to see how well it can predict. And so Jerome and Jay began to publish *Industry Forecast*, a monthly report that analyzes and forecasts business conditions. As the years went by, people did take notice.

Jerome died in 1967, a few days before his eighty-fifth birthday. We, Jerome's son and grandson, now write the *Forecast*, which continues to compile an enviable record of reliability. When an editorial in *Barron's* in September 1980 said, "S Jay Levy whose track record on business ups and downs is matchless," the editor was effectively paying tribute to Jerome Levy and 70 years of productive economic research.

Today, people around the world are wrestling with unemployment and inflation. Dismaying economic problems persist despite the great expansion of economic knowledge since Taft's address at Cooper Union. During the seven decades that have elapsed since Jerome discovered the sources of profits, many economists have made important contributions to their field, but they have paid too little attention to profits, the lifeblood of capitalism.

The inability of even affluent nations to solve their economic problems is a threat to capitalism and democracy. We have observed with concern the disenchantment with rising prices, mounting unemployment, and slipping standard of living that led France to shift sharply toward socialism in 1981. We are worried about the economic distress in Britain and its possibly dire consequences for the survival of free enterprise in that country. Our apprehension is heightened by our conviction that a successful capitalist economy is a prerequisite for a free society.

Our goal in writing this book is to correct serious misunderstandings about the poor performance of our country's economy. Chronic unemployment and incessant inflation are largely the results of people acting on misconceptions. Myths and erroneous beliefs about profits are especially destructive.

Capitalism is inherently a just and extraordinarily productive system, but when it is badly abused by ignorant or venal governments, its performance is poor and its distribution of income grossly inequitable. When properly run, the system gives everyone both the opportunity to work and a fair share of the nation's product. Indeed, our system can provide full employment and, at the same time, successfully deal with inflation.

Serious economic challenges and great opportunities lie ahead for America. We can meet the challenges and take advantage of the opportunities if the leaders of government and the public at large understand our economy—its capabilities, its workings and its limitations. Our hope is that this book will contribute to the understanding of capitalism that Americans need in order to support policies that will save our economy and preserve our freedom.

Profits and the Future of American Society

# 1

# Profits and the Future
# of American Society

*Profit!* That word stirs up controversy. It means many things to different people and sometimes many things to one person. To some it is a dirty word, a synonym for stolen goods, wealth filched from workers. To others it signifies opportunity, initiative, and freedom.

Most people, whether they think profits are good or bad, will consider this definition acceptable: Profits are the excess of business revenues over business expenses. Accountants will be quick to point out that this statement leaves a lot of technical issues open, but it suffices to give us a common, basic understanding of what profits are. We will use this definition throughout the book, elaborating on it as the need arises.

Most Americans, especially those who derive substantial income from profits, think that profits are good. Still, they often harbor subconscious doubts about the morality of these gains and feel pressed to justify their affluence.

*Are* profits immoral? Do they flow along some shady path from the pockets of upstanding citizens into the hands of parasitic individuals? You will be hard pressed to find out just how profits originate if you seek the answer in even a distinguished library. Because almost all the best-known economic theorists have concentrated their efforts on investigating other questions, the sources of profits have remained obscure. We will discover that profits are *not* inherently immoral, but only after we see how they are generated.

Once we know more about profits—where they come from, what

they do, and how they affect the economy—"profit" will no longer be a perplexing or disturbing word. We will recognize that profits are inherent in any economic system, and that they are as essential to private enterprise as gasoline is to the operation of automobiles.

In the 1970s, the flow of profits—this fuel for our economic engine—was uneven and frequently inadequate. As a result, our profit-motivated economy did not perform well. Employment, investment in new plant and equipment, and the nation's standard of living were all disappointing. Meanwhile, inflation changed from a minor annoyance to a serious affliction and was found by public-opinion pollsters to be the nation's most serious economic problem.

Americans are all too aware of how policymakers in Washington have attempted to find remedies for our economic ills. Year after year, officials proposed new legislation. When a scheme was strongly supported, a congressional committee weighed its merits. The committee's hearings seldom clarified the issue.

Typically, economists and other experts testify at congressional hearings, often as representatives of various industries, labor unions, banks, consumers, and so forth. Frequently, half of them agree that the proposed legislation will help our economy, while the other half assert that it will be harmful. An observer has to believe that the witnesses on at least one side of the argument do not know what they are talking about. And he cannot be sure that their opponents do either.

During the 1970s, many economists prescribed monetary stringency and fiscal restraint in order to control inflation and promote prosperity. Although some efforts, perhaps feeble ones, were made to apply these remedies, inflation showed few, if any, signs of being cured. Unemployment became more of a serious problem and the standard of living no longer seemed to rise.

The 1980s arrived accompanied by a growing conviction among influential Americans that the federal government must resolutely strive to control and balance its budget. They also believed, perhaps more firmly, that the Federal Reserve had to exercise an iron will in order to limit the growth of the nation's money supply. The fiscal aims proved to be elusive while monetary restraint managed to reduce the rate of inflation—but at a cost. The Federal Reserve's efforts to restrain the use of credit interfered with the vital process of generating profits. By seriously curtailing the amount of profits in the economy, monetary policy set a record of sorts: it caused two recessions in two years. Credit restraint also brought levels of unemployment unacceptable to anyone, the highest bankruptcy rate since World War II, and even the revival of a term that had not been in wide use for forty years: "depression." Moreover, the Federal Reserve's strategy made a balanced federal budget a virtual impossibility.

The doctors of the economy who prescribe monetary and fiscal remedies for inflation are prone to blame the politicians for not properly administering the medicine. Yet the doctors have erred. In making their diagnosis, they have mistaken the symptoms for the disease. They have seen inflation and the lack of economic growth as problems in and of themselves, brought on by government's mistakes. They have failed to see that our economic problems arise from deeply ingrained attitudes that are embodied in powerful institutions as well as from demographic, technological, sociological, and environmental changes that have altered the basic nature of both American and world economies.

Our economy is functioning in a climate that subjects it to new and intensifying strains. The world's expanding population and industrialization are the chief causes of this adverse development. The number of human beings on Earth is expected to be five times as large in the year 2000 as it was in 1900. This growth has, more than any other change, led to scarcities and high costs of materials, especially energy. The world will have quintupled its need for food within the twentieth century. In the United States, a growing population of older people is already unsettling and threatening to overwhelm the social security system. Under these circumstances, the economy is going to encounter increasing difficulty in fulfilling the expectations of the American people.

Profits, the phenomenon that motivates most of the production in a private-enterprise economy, must receive more attention if we are to cope successfully with the challenges ahead. Indeed, to understand profits is to understand the operation of the economy. One can achieve a much better focus on inflation, unemployment, and other maladies with knowledge of what determines the aggregate profitability of American business and how profits affect business behavior.

Surprisingly, profits have never been in vogue among economists or politicians as a focal point for policies or for diagnosing economic conditions. Instead, discussions of economic matters in this century have been dominated by views that fine-tuning national income, optimizing the size and growth rate of the money supply, or balancing the federal government's budget is the proper course to pursue in order to attain prosperity. Washington has never even considered trying to ensure that the economy generate the right amount of profits as an approach to managing the economy.

Our focus on profits should not seem peculiar. Profits are virtually the sole motivation for business to employ people, buy new machines, conduct research, produce goods and services, and so forth. They are the overriding reason why private enterprises exist; without them, no business can survive for long. And, of course, if employers could not make profits, business would provide no jobs. The American economic system depends on profits. Few persons can afford to maintain a business "just for fun."

The power of profits to motivate productive efforts was given a noteworthy demonstration at the beginning of American history. Jamestown, Virginia, which was established in 1607, became the first successful English colony in what is now the United States. However, it was not immediately a success; dissension, famine, disease, and conflicts with the Indians almost led to its abandonment. For ten years it was barely able to survive and would have succumbed had it not received sizable infusions of supplies and manpower from England.

The original settlers were employees of the Virginia Company with no stake in the profitability of the venture. Not until these men became tenant farmers and landowners did Jamestown secure its destiny. As employees, the colonists accomplished nothing; as entrepreneurs, motivated by the opportunity for profit, they built a prosperous, strong community.

After Jamestown had become successful, Captain John Smith looked back upon its earlier history and noted, "When our people were fed out of the common store, and laboured jointly together, glad was he who could slip from his labour, or slumber over his taske, he cared not how; nay, the most honest among them would hardly take so much true paines in a week, as now for themselves they will doe in a day." *

The history of the early and subsequent achievements of the American economy is the story of people who profited while they were building one industry after another—the inland water transportation, farm machinery, railroad, steel, photography, automobile, aluminum, chain store, computer, fast food, and many other industries. Profits were a superb motivator of the innovation and enterprise that continually increased the standard of living.

Profits are so fundamental to our system that an understanding of them is necessary in order to properly interpret changes in gross national product, the money supply, and other gauges of activity in the economy. One would expect that any serious treatment of economics must emphasize the role of profits. Indeed, microeconomics, the study of the functioning of the individual firm and the individual industry, is dominated by the concept that the sole, or at least primary, motivation for anything that a company does is profit maximization.

But strangely, in macroeconomics, which is concerned with the entire economy—with such issues as unemployment, inflation, and industrial growth—the consideration of profits all but vanishes. The tradition that emphasizes the importance of profits in many parts of the system but tends to overlook their role in the health of the whole is passed on from one generation of economists to the next. "Profit" isn't even in the indexes of some well-regarded macroeconomic textbooks.

The versions of macroeconomics taught in our institutions of

* Captain John Smith as quoted by Samuel Eliot Morison in the *Oxford History of the American People* (New York: Oxford University Press, 1965), p. 52.

higher learning implicitly assume that strong business profitability is a characteristic or consequence of economic prosperity rather than a cause. This notion is reminiscent of the Ptolemaic theory of astronomy. Centuries ago, people believed that all heavenly bodies revolved around the earth. This notion led them to the conclusion that the other planets moved on peculiar paths. To explain their movements from the geocentric view of the universe requires a fertile imagination; to describe them requires complicated equations. However, once the actual physics of the solar system is recognized, planetary motion becomes relatively logical and simple. Similarly, recognizing the center of our economic system eliminates the mystery and complexity that inhibit understanding.

Economics becomes a more powerful science when observations about the economy can be put into proper perspective. The view afforded by an understanding of profits is more revealing than those views provided by the mainstream of modern economic thought.

Underlying much of mainstream economics is the work of John Maynard Keynes. Keynesian theory focuses on the level of *total spending* in the economy—that is, the total amount spent by consumers, government, business (for investment), and foreigners. (Keynesians also talk about *total income.*) Too much spending will cause inflation; too little will result in unemployment. Lord Keynes, who contributed so much to the discipline of economics, said nothing explicitly about the sources of profits or how the aggregate amount of profits in the economy affects prosperity.

The other major influence on mainstream economics is monetarism, which concerns itself with the effects of changes in the total amount of money in the economy. Orthodox monetarists say that the steady growth of the money supply at a reasonable rate is the *sole* prerequisite for a healthy capitalist economy. As long as such a rate of growth is maintained, the monetarists believe, free markets will take care of prices, interest rates, and employment. Monetarism says little about profits.

The simultaneous presence of inflation and unemployment in the 1970s is an outstanding example of a phenomenon that can be correctly understood from the profit perspective, but not with

Keynesian or monetarist theory. These schools blame rising prices on too much total spending and on too much growth of the money supply, respectively. But they explain unemployment as the consequence of *too little* spending or *too little* monetary growth. The co-existence of these two disorders in recent years has been referred to as a "paradox" and has been labeled "stagflation."

From the profit perspective, inflation can arise from a number of causes. For example, in 1966, an ill-advised government deficit unleashed a major inflationary force. In 1980, the principal forces behind inflation included the rising price of imported petroleum and increasing labor costs, *not* the government's fiscal policy. In that year, inflation and unemployment were problems with unrelated causes.

Monetarism cannot make these distinctions. It cannot adequately explain a complex, modern economy in a changing world. Keynesian theory also has difficulty coping with new influences on our economy.

Many members of these dominant schools of economic thought have amended their basic premises in an effort to cope with the realities of the modern world. In the shadow of their failure to adequately explain recent economic difficulties and offer acceptable remedies, a plethora of cranks and fly-by-night theoreticians have taken advantage of Americans' disillusionment and longing for some answers.

Economic analysts have been generating volumes of information as they strive to better understand vexing problems. In view of the controversy about which measures of economic performance matter—not to mention what they all mean—an observer can easily be overwhelmed by the facts and figures available. So many data are supplied by government, media, and private analysts that interpreting them, or even weeding out what is unimportant, seems a Herculean task. For example, "money supply" has had at least eleven definitions in recent years. The names given to these concepts of money supply are: M1, M1+, M1-A, M1-B, M1-B shift adjusted, M2, M3, M4, M5, M6, and even L. And the job market? There are two primary sets of employment figures (which often behave differently) and all

kinds of unemployment indexes, including a survey of the thick-
nesses of "want ad" sections across the nation. All of the better-
known price indexes, which frequently give different evaluations of
inflation, are regularly criticized, and some of the critics have been
busy developing alternative indexes that make inflation appear to
be much less severe or much worse. In the course of a month, a
reader of the *Wall Street Journal* and the *Journal of Commerce* will
encounter a plethora of sales figures, surveys of consumer and business intentions, as well as statistics on construction, new orders,
profits, interest rates, consumer credit, foreign transaction balances,
exchange rates, gold prices, oil prices, steel prices, auto prices,
stock prices, wage rates, the government's budget, production, productivity, etc., etc. . . . not to mention revisions of earlier data.

All of these numbers reveal something, but how can anyone concerned about the general health of the economy know which to
focus on, and then how to make sense out of this information? The
problem is challenging under any circumstances, but when one understands profits and sees them in the correct perspective, one can
more readily see the relevance of various statistics for answering a
special critical question. For example, one can determine with a
high degree of confidence what the effect of an increase in business
debt to banks, or of a decrease in federal grants to local governments, will be on corporate profits, inflation, and unemployment.
Forecasting becomes much less chancy.

The modern way to deal with vast quantities of data, the production of which is greatly facilitated by computers, is to stuff them
back into a computer. Too often people without a clear perspective
on the operation of the economy seek to use their machines to
search for statistical relationships in hope that they will thus discover secret truths about how our system operates. Certainly computers
have many important applications, but they cannot produce expla-
nations of economic phenomena if the human beings directing
them lack fundamental understanding of how the economy works.

Fortunately, the operation of the economy is not nearly as complicated as the confused state of economics might lead one to be-

lieve. Even those bewildered by the jargon and equations of the "experts" are in their own right more expert than they realize. Nearly every adult American has the knowledge that comes from actual experience: working for compensation, consuming, borrowing, lending, and saving. We know about making and liquidating investments, giving to charities, paying taxes and insurance premiums. In the course of a year, each one of us is probably engaged in almost every type of transaction that occurs in our economy.

What one individual does is not too difficult to understand. However, the economy seems complex because so many others are doing the same thing. But most transactions simply subtract money from one purse and add it to another. Just because many tens of millions of people are involved does not make the economy or the principles governing its operation incomprehensible.

The economic activities with which Americans are most concerned—pricing and employing—are not mysterious. They are by and large performed by the firms, great and small, that comprise the business community. The fundamentals of why these firms hire, fire, cut prices, or boost them, why a consumer buys or saves, and why a worker wants a raise are not beyond the layman's understanding. After all, he has firsthand knowledge on these matters.

For example, we can investigate the problem of inflation by asking direct questions in everyday language that virtually anyone can understand. Why do prices rise? Because sellers raise them. Why do they raise them? Either to increase their profit margins or to protect margins following an increase in operating costs. Why do these costs rise? What determines profit margins? We can—and will—answer these questions without resorting to complicated mathematics or computer analyses.

Unfortunately, too many people are asking the wrong questions altogether. If everybody in the country approached the problem of inflation from the perspective suggested above, the real causes of rising prices would be widely known. However, we live in a time of little common understanding and we read and hear a great deal of economic nonsense. The rhetoric that purports to explain inflation makes a lengthy list. Some of it is valid; most is not.

"Too many dollars chasing too few goods!"

"An overheated economy!"

"The wage-price spiral!"

"Inflationary expectations!"

"Fiscal irresponsibility!"

"Government has gotten too big!"

"OPEC!"

"We lack the discipline of the gold standard!"

"Consumers are borrowing too much, saving too little!"

. . . and so on.

The inadequate understanding of profits makes economic policymaking and forecasting extremely hazardous. Politics, which readily engulfs any important issue characterized by even the slightest uncertainty, further complicates the job of managing our economy. The result is ill-conceived government manipulations that weaken the economy, deprive people of jobs, reduce the standard of living, and discourage investment in plant and equipment—even when the intent is to produce precisely the opposite results.

But poor government policymaking is only part of the cost of Americans' misunderstanding of the operation of their economic system. Myths about profits, economic problems, and even the basic relationships between employer and employee, worker and consumer, and consumer and consumer, cause people to behave in ways that injure society. Their actions lower the national standard of living, obscure national objectives, and produce unnecessary social tensions.

Consider the following statements:

- An increase in total wages will decrease total profits in the economy.
- Conversely, if business were to succeed in reducing the average wage, the saving would be reflected in higher profits.
- As the preceding statements imply, the real fight for larger portions of the economic pie is between labor and capitalists.
- A large portion of the consumer goods produced in the United States is bought by persons with their income from profits,

leaving significantly fewer goods for consumers whose income is wages and salaries.

- Profits do not reflect any real contribution to the production process.
- The total amount of profits in an economy depends on business's greed.
- Socialist and Communist countries can successfully eliminate profits, and have.

None of these statements is new. Vast numbers of people subscribe to each one of them. Furthermore, all of them have a common attribute—not one is true.

Even if economists know that these notions are false, many of them fall prey to others which, at best, are misleading.

- Inflation is responsible for eroding the average American's standard of living.
- Inflation in the Seventies and Eighties is the result of federal deficit spending and/or lax monetary policies.
- Periodic recessions are inevitable.
- Recessions can cure modern inflation.

Among the myths about profits is that of the class struggle between capitalists and the proletariat, described so effectively by Karl Marx. Even many supporters of private enterprise believe that the basic interests of employers and employees are opposed to each other. Seldom is this concept of the economy questioned by those who observe that prosperity does not visit capitalists and labor alternatively, but falls upon both of them simultaneously.

The class-struggle myth is destructive. It adds friction to the process of production. Employers and employees are encouraged to be antagonists toward each other. Cooperation is impeded, and productivity suffers. Americans produce fewer of the goods and services that satisfy their needs and desires, and their economy is less able to compete in international markets.

Myths are not a sound basis for national policies. For democracy to work, citizens need to have at least a minimal understanding of the questions they vote on. When issues involving choices of economic policy arise, this prerequisite for government of, by, and for the people is appallingly lacking. Politicians seize upon economic ideas and present them to the electorate. The voters, understandably confused and distrustful of economic promises, are in a quandary.

In the long run, the very existence of our system may be threatened by growing doubts and fears about Washington's ability to make constructive economic decisions. A frightened public is not resistant to the politicians' prescriptions, be they well-intentioned cures or demagogic nostrums. Some of the economic remedies offered today are no better than the cure-all potions once sold by peddlers who never unhitched their horses until they were well out of town.

If profits are so central, so crucial to the operation of the economy, and, on top of it all, so fundamental, how can it be that they have been so slighted? We cannot answer this question confidently.

Could it be that this oversight has its roots in the ethical traditions of Western civilization? Individuals who become economists are often motivated by their ideals. Many of them dream of curing some dreadful disease of our society. They hope to eliminate poverty or end abuses of power. Yet perhaps their preconceived notions about the morality of profits prevent them from taking an unbiased look. Whether they are religious or not, they have grown up in a society whose ethics reflect the biblical association of wealth with abuses of power. In the Old Testament, Isaiah proclaims:

> The Lord will enter into judgment
> With the elders of His people,
>   and the princes thereof:
> "It is ye that have eaten up the vineyard;
> The spoil of the poor is in your houses;
> what mean ye that ye crush My people,
> And grind the face of the poor?"
> Saith the Lord, the God of hosts. (Isaiah 3:14–15)

No prophet of revolutionary socialism ever used more eloquent rhetoric than this biblical advocate of justice.

Profits have always been associated with wealth, and rich people have been subject to moral condemnation for thousands of years. That God is sometimes addressed as "Father of the poor" says a lot about how Western religion often views affluence. For nearly two millennia, many preachers have derived inspiration and the poor have drawn solace from the often-cited statement "How hard it is for the wealthy to enter the kingdom of God!"

Before the end of the nineteenth century, the places of the "elders and the princes" had been taken, in the eyes of Marxists and many other socialists, by the capitalists. To this day, revolutionaries claim that the capitalist is a despicable parasite who steals his profits from his employees. When the modern capitalist is pictured as a rich vampire who feeds on the blood of workers, an ancient idea is being restated.

So perhaps our religious and cultural heritage has dissuaded economists from looking squarely at profits. Who knows? But certainly the notion that profits per se are sinful dwells in many a subconscious.

Both the current state of the economy and the problems that must be faced between now and the end of the century are disturbing. To make matters worse, many Americans have exaggerated ideas about the present capability of their economy. Their unrealistic expectations increase the difficulty of overcoming the challenges that lie ahead.

The United States economy has enormous strength despite the abuse it has received from its people and government. When governed and governors alike begin to understand their economic system and face the challenges ahead realistically, Americans can save their economy. We can prosper.

# 2

# The Challenge of 2000

Almost everyone wants to have a big slice of that famous dish, the economic pie—the culinary metaphor for the economy's output of consumer goods and services. In the 1950s and 1960s, rising employment and increasing worker productivity brought the nation successively larger pies; almost everyone had the pleasure of consuming a larger slice each year. However, in the 1970s, the annual improvements became smaller, until the average portion of the pie—the national standard of living—actually began to decrease.

*The purpose of an economy is to produce consumer goods and services efficiently and to distribute them in accordance with some principle of fairness.* When the American economy doesn't produce as much as it should, we are dissatisfied. When some people are receiving slices of pie that are undeservedly large or inexcusably small, we are indignant—especially if we count ourselves among the deprived. At the beginning of the 1980s, most Americans thought that our economy was not adequately fulfilling its purpose.

Despite reasonably close agreement on the economy's purpose, the views on how to achieve it vary widely. Some people firmly believe that a high rate of personal saving or trade unions or tight control of the money supply are essential to the satisfactory operation of the economy. But these and other institutions and practices do not necessarily help to achieve more production or an equitable distribution of the national product.

How big the pie is depends first on the number of people who

14

are employed. Two workers will produce twice as much as one. If they work 40 hours a week, they will ordinarily produce one-third more than if they work only 30 hours.

The size of the pie also depends on how productive the workers are. Inept, lazy people using poor tools cannot match the output of eager, skillful workers using the most advanced equipment.

A previously insignificant phenomenon is now seriously and adversely affecting the size of the American economic pie. In order to produce goods and services, the United States needs to import materials—it has to trade extensively with foreign nations. The prices of some of the imported materials have increased faster than domestic prices. Thus our terms of trade have worsened. For example, we have to give five times as much of our real national product as we did in 1970 in order to obtain one barrel of oil. During the Seventies, increasingly unfavorable terms of trade for petroleum and many other basic materials reduced the availability of goods and services to our own consumers.

Whatever the size of the economic pie, it must be distributed. Anyone who ever sat at the table when mother's apple pie arrived understands the problem. An eager little boy with an elastic appetite learned something about economics when he eyed the whole dessert, looked around the table to see who was there—mother, father, sister, brother, and, perhaps, a guest or two—and estimated how big a slice of the pie he would get. Two guests made a difference in its size!

Mother divided the pie in accordance with her principles. She may have served an identical slice to each diner. Or she may have given each person a portion that represented his or her capacity—a small one for little sister, the largest for father.

In the United States, the economic pie is divided without much premeditation. However, most Americans know that the system is supposed to reward "each according to his or her contribution to production." The more a person's efforts increase the economic output, the larger his purchasing power should be. To reward people on any other basis would not encourage them to be productive. If incomes depended on one's knowledge of classical languages, many people would study Greek and Latin rather than work hard at producing products or services. Souls might benefit at the expense of stomachs.

Increases in income are not always rewards for contributions to production. In the United States today, a worker's compensation may rise if she joins a union. A surgeon's income increases when he performs an unnecessary operation. A mechanic receives a smaller raise than her coworkers because of her sex.

"To each according to what he can get" is the operating principle. Hopefully, the market equates what a person can get for his services with what he contributes to production. Often it does. A railroad engineer earns more in a week than a supermarket clerk, because, in society's view, safely driving thousands of tons of train and cargo to their destination adds more to the economic pie than bagging groceries. Throughout the economy, commissions, bonuses, and promotions to higher-paying jobs are usually based on performance—on contributions to production.

The "to each according to what he can get" attitude has become a powerful inflationary force in the American economy since the mid-1960s, because the market is frequently *not* doing its job. As individuals, union members, and members of professional associations, we have become more adept at obtaining higher compensations than at enlarging the economic pie. Workers are continually being given more money for the same performance. (By "workers" we mean everyone who is compensated for doing a job, from the president of the United States to the chairman of General Motors to the person who empties the wastebaskets.)

The output of consumer goods and services is going to have a difficult time growing during the 1980s. Making the pie bigger has become a problem. For a variety of reasons, American productivity has been improving slowly if at all.

Most of the rise in gross national product during the 1970s was attributable to the growth of the labor force. The United States' GNP increased because the postwar babies were becoming adults and significantly augmenting the working population. Furthermore, women, who had formerly remained close to the hearth, were streaming into industry and commerce. But the output per person, which was previously the biggest factor in economic growth, merely edged upward.

The future growth of the labor force will be much slower than it was in the 1970s. It will reflect the dwindling birthrate of the 1960s and 1970s and the virtual completion of the migration of women from homes to offices and factories; most adult females are already in the labor force. Meanwhile, productivity is not likely to improve greatly in the decade of the 1980s, for reasons we will discuss later on.

The standard of living depends not only on the size of the economic pie but also on how many people are at the table. In the years ahead, the number of consumers may increase faster than the size of the pie, largely because of greater longevity. Already in the United States, the ratio of active workers to retired ones is 4:1. The population of retirees is growing much faster than the work force. In 50 years the ratio is likely to be less than 3:1—unless most people work long after their sixty-fifth birthdays.

Successive declines in the average standard of living are the result of too little growth in the output of goods and services and of too fast an expansion in the number of consumers. Disappointment, even anger, over these declines sustains and exacerbates inflation. When the system seems to be cheating them, people strive to get more money in order to have larger portions of economic pie. Their efforts bring higher salaries, wages, fees, commissions, etc. These increased compensations add directly to business costs, forcing prices to rise. Yet no one is necessarily producing more.

As long as workers are disappointed with their standard of living and fight for higher wages and salaries without doing more work, a serious inflationary force will endure. Until people begin to understand the difficulties in increasing output in the decades ahead, the outlook for price stability will not be encouraging.

The once fairly dependable relationship of money to the economic pie has been shattered. Consider the case of the truck driver who was asked in 1981 if he would be happy to earn $90,000 in 1996. He wisely ducked the question. When he was asked if he would be happy to earn enough in 1996 to live in an eight-room, single-family house, eat steak twice a week, belong to a health club, have a library of tapes for his video recorder, and send his children to college, he confidently answered, "Yes."

People once depended on money in a way that is no longer realistic. They could save it for years and find that it had lost little value. Now, if they hold money for ten years, it may lose most of its purchasing power.

Although inflation is hardly desirable, it does not erode the standard of living. The declining consumer purchasing power of recent years was the result of higher costs of imported energy and other materials, an absence of productivity gains, and greater longevity. Inflation does not reduce the standard of living; to a considerable degree, the disappointing standard of living leads to inflation.

Although inflation has barely any effect on the size of the pie, it has a significant effect on how it is sliced. Inflation reduces the portions of many of those who spend money that they previously saved. Increasing longevity is expanding the proportion of the population that lives on savings—older people who are likely to be at least semiretired. After the year 2000, and especially during the decade of the 2020s, this group will be making huge claims on the economic pie. The number of people 65 years old and older will more than double between 1980 and 2030. If these senior citizens obtain what they now believe they will be entitled to, the active workers who produce the economic pie had better be highly productive, much more so than at present. If they are not, these creators of the national product will have to learn to tolerate slim slices as their compensations. The alternative will be a fierce economic struggle between active and retired workers—a war between generations.

We were accustomed to living in a world of plenty, but we are now in a world of scarcity. From the beginning of the Industrial Revolution until about 1973, nature was generous. The human race, especially in America, had all the resources it wanted and needed. The challenge was how to use them to make desirable goods. Now the challenge is often how to find materials, how to find substitutes, how to stretch what we have. The task ahead will become more difficult. The era of scarcity has only begun.

At the root of the aggravated problems of the new era will be a staggering expansion of the number of human beings, which was little more than 1 billion in 1900. Demographers warn us that the population of the world, which increased 40% from 1960 to 1980, will rise another 40% by the year 2000. Earth's people, who now number 4 billion, will, these experts say, total 6 billion.

By 2000, 35 million more Americans will be alive than in 1980. In some countries—for example, Mexico, Pakistan, and Brazil— populations, according to demographers, will have doubled in these 20 years.

Maybe the experts are wrong. A surge in the use of contraceptives, or starvation, may limit the world's population growth to 1 billion people during the final two decades of the century. But even 1 billion additional people in an increasingly industrialized world will make vastly augmented demands on the available resources. Earth, as a consequence, will provide many materials only at greater cost than at present. Mines will be dug deeper, poor ores will be exploited, fishermen will stay longer at sea to search for elusive catches, and farmers will till land that is now considered unsuitable for agriculture. The world of scarcity is one in which more machinery and more work will be required than in 1980 to obtain a hundred pounds of cod, a barrel of oil, a ton of copper, and so forth.

The dual challenge of the approaching twenty-first century is to increase production while using resources sparingly. And what is being done? A good part of the industrial world has adopted economic policies designed to restrain production. As a result, unemployment becomes worse, and investments in the new plant and equipment that are needed, if we are to successfully meet the challenge of the future, are not being made.

What can we do to raise the standard of living in an era when the scarcity of many important materials will increasingly challenge the nation's ability to make bigger economic pies? What can we do when a growing number of retirees increases the probability that the pie may be continually divided into smaller slices?

The first step is to put the primary focus on profits. Our economy can almost always have an optimum amount of profits, one that induces private industry to produce the maximum amount of goods and services. To obtain these profits, business will, as it has always done when it sensed opportunities for gain, increase both its investment in the most efficient plant and equipment and its employment of workers.

To meet the challenge of 2000, the economy must put available people to work, encourage them to work as many hours a week as is reasonable, and provide them with the most efficient tools to perform their tasks. Business can be induced to do this job. It needs adequate profit incentives.

The economic successes that have been recorded in history leave little doubt about the power of profits to work wonders. The dismal failures of Soviet collective farms, the near demise of Jamestown and its subsequent success, and the exciting accomplishments of a host of American corporations argue strongly for capitalism. The profit motive can be credited for the marvelous, innovative contributions made to American consumers by private enterprise—for example, Woolworth in the 1900s, Ford in the 1910s and 1920s, Dupont and Minnesota Mining in the 1930s, McDonald's, Xerox, Zenith, and Polaroid in the post–World War II era. Nothing matches the ability of profits to encourage the translation of ideas into additional economic output.

As we remove the mystery from profits, we will reveal that changes in wages and salaries are unsuitable devices for improving the distribution of income between employers and employees. An increase in the rate of compensation for one group of workers is at the expense of other workers and retirees. Similarly, losses incurred by some corporations become profits of others. Once enough people have an understanding of the relationships between wage rates and profits and the purchasing power of savings, inflation can be successfully tackled. But prevailing concepts make it impossible for Americans to make any lasting headway against the trend of rapidly rising prices.

# 3

# How a Marxist Myth Hurts America

"The history of all hitherto existing society is the history of class struggles," wrote Karl Marx in 1848. He was, of course, especially interested in a struggle between the proletariat and the capitalists. As he saw it, the capitalists would dominate and exploit their employees until the downtrodden workers could rally to destroy their oppressors.

If you ask the first person you see walking down an American street whether he or she is a Marxist, the odds are overwhelming that the answer will be "No." With some individuals, you would ingratiate yourself no less by asking if they are thieves. To be sure, most Americans are *not* disciples of the nineteenth-century economist-philosopher, yet their words and actions reflect a belief in the employer-employee "struggle" that he stridently described. Relatively few people believe in a class war for dominance, but vast numbers see the contests between individual workers and their bosses over compensation rates as part of an ongoing tug-of-war in which workers and "business" both try to get more of the economic pie at the other's expense. They assume that if all wages and salaries in the economy increased, total profits would decrease, and workers would enjoy a higher standard of living. *They are wrong*. The widely accepted notion that changes in pay rates affect the distribution of income between employees as a class and the owners of business as a class is a myth!

Unfortunately, this myth is not a harmless idiosyncrasy of the

American culture. It is a source of injustice and inefficiency that costs the nation dearly. The worker-capitalist (or worker-business, or employee-employer) class-struggle myth and the damage it does warrant our attention.

American politics reflect our society's belief in the battle between classes. In Washington, business lobbyists oppose labor lobbies on many issues. Presidents, congressmen, election results, and legislation are frequently labeled "pro-business" or "pro-labor." Herbert Hoover was on business's side. Republicans are regularly hailed by business people as their allies. Franklin Roosevelt was "a friend of labor." Democrats frequently claim that the support of blue-collar voters is their birthright. Politicians seeking endorsements from both "labor" and "business" constituencies know that they must carefully balance their appeals.

Underlying all the rhetoric on both sides of the labor-versus-business debates is the belief that a trade-off exists between worker compensation and profits. If one rises, people assume, the other must fall. They correctly note that if *one* company raises its wages, its profits suffer. They naturally assume that the same relationship holds for the whole private economy. It does not.

*An increase in the average wage causes an approximately proportionate rise in profits.* We will not verify this statement until we have explained the sources of profits, but we can observe immediately that it is consistent with economic history: the long-term trends of corporate profits and worker compensation move up and down *together*. If wages and salaries were paid at the expense of profits, profits would fall when pay rose, and rise when compensation declined.

The above assertion about the relationship between wages and profits may be hard to swallow at first, but it becomes plausible if we look at an example of a pay increase won by some workers and its consequences. In the 1970s, a department-store worker did not gain from the victory of fellow laborers when the United Auto Workers won a raise. He lost. He celebrated their success by paying a higher price for their products, American automobiles. Why? Because when UAW wages increased, American automakers raised their prices in an effort to maintain profitability. Indeed, all employees who bought American cars lost real purchasing power. These losses were their contributions to their fellow workers who were UAW members. The auto workers increased their own ability to purchase economic pie, but they reduced the portions available to other workers. The UAW raise was not the one-sided victory for labor that a casual observer might have thought it was.

Meanwhile, the higher prices charged by the domestic auto producers for their cars discouraged some customers. A number of them bought imported vehicles. Others did not purchase any autos. Profits declined. Within the domestic auto industry, labor indeed triumphed over business.

But many firms enjoyed increased profits! Once the auto workers had higher incomes, they spent more. The proprietors of taverns and restaurants in downtown Detroit and the owners of other establishments that sold to auto workers were in buoyant spirits. Their cash registers rang more often. Some of these businessmen were even able to increase prices. Their profits improved.

As the effects of the auto workers' pay raise rippled through the economy, they cast doubt on the concept that higher wages benefit workers at the expense of the owners of business. Certainly the workers gained at the expense of business within the auto industry. However, business gained and workers lost outside the auto industry.

*Generally, a pay increase will have virtually no effect on the division of the economic pie between the "capitalist class" and the "working class."* One group of workers may increase its purchasing power at the expense of other workers, or workers generally may gain at the expense of retirees living on savings. However, if total wages in the economy rise, ordinarily so will profits. (While the wage increase in the UAW example above did not cut directly into profits, it did weaken the United States' competitive position in the world auto market. As a result, America fared worse in international trade, and profits were lost to Japan, West Germany, and other nations.)

Another reason to doubt that the interests of business and labor are mutually opposed is the historic relationship between profits and employment. Growth in employment accompanies increases in profits. During the early 1930s, profits vanished and employment plummeted. In the latter years of that decade, profits recovered some of the ground lost between 1929 and 1932. Employment rose, although not enough to make a big dent in unemployment. When World War II came, profits soared, employment expanded, and the jobless virtually disappeared. In subsequent years, prosperity did not visit business and workers alternately. Good times and recessions were experienced by employers and employees simultaneously.

This evidence does not argue well for a conflict of interest between capitalists and workers. As a matter of fact, the similarities in the trends of profits and employment are no coincidence. More profits in the economy *cause* business to expand its payrolls. We will argue that policies designed to optimize the aggregate amount of profits are the key to eliminating unemployment. Yet many people persist in believing in a trade-off between the prosperity of business and the well-being of the employees in our society. This myth affects attitudes on factory floors, at labor union meetings, in executive offices, in barrooms, and, of course, in legislative chambers.

Widespread belief in a capitalist-worker class struggle hampers the equitable distribution of the economic pie. This fallacious concept can justify almost any means employees may adopt to fight for higher pay. But because increased compensation does not benefit the working class at the expense of business, the unrestrained pursuit of raises results in workers vying *with one another* for purchasing power. It also pits active workers against retirees and other people who depend on savings. These contests often cause the economic pie to be distributed unfairly, even cruelly.

The acceptance of the employee-employer class struggle also conceals a real, serious conflict between workers and consumers. Even though workers are also consumers, a struggle between these two groups exists. Most people desire to work less and consume more. Yet less work means less is produced for consumption. This natural conflict of desires is evident when consumers demand a higher standard of living, and workers demand shorter hours. Because workers are paid by business, and consumers buy from business, people often blame business when they are dissatisfied with the purchasing power they receive for work they do.

How can people think that they can work less and consume more? Because the relationship between work and consumption is not clear in our modern economy. The real value of most employees' work has become obscure.

How much pie does a day's work produce? In a simple society, the answer is usually quite obvious. The simplest economy we can think of was that of Robinson Crusoe, the ill-fated traveler who was shipwrecked alone on a tropical island by a ferocious storm and the pen of Daniel Defoe. Defoe, himself a writer on economic subjects, described Crusoe's one-man economy in great detail.

Robinson Crusoe could not forget that his standard of living was entirely dependent on his work. He knew that he had to balance his conflicting desires to consume and to have leisure. He never said, "I should have twice as many fish, a canoe, and a new shirt. And I should also have Saturday off and two fifteen-minute raisin breaks every day." These demands for more consumption and less work would have made no sense to Crusoe because he knew how much economic pie he created each hour or day that he worked. For one day's work, he might earn six fish, a leg for his new stool, or two armfuls of fruit. He knew exactly what he produced.

But a production worker on a Ford assembly line, a lawyer in the company's patent department, and a file clerk in its public-relations office do not have clear ideas of how much pie they respectively create during a day's work. They do not know how to evaluate their efforts in terms of refrigerators, books, hamburgers, down jackets, and dental floss—things they want to buy. In a modern economy, workers are so specialized that they can no longer see a relationship between their work and their purchasing power.

Even the assembly worker cannot judge what portion of the value of a completed automobile—his own company's product—represents his contribution. He has little idea of how many total hours of work go into the manufacture of a car—including the hours of workers at steel mills, chemical plants, parts manufacturers, and railroad yards. The lawyer and the file clerk have an even more hopeless task if they try to calculate their contributions to each car.

Most employees in our economy have the same problem as the three Ford employees: They do not know how much they contribute to the economic pie. They know what their paychecks can buy, but they cannot tell whether their living standards accurately reflect their contributions.

Since the operation of the United States economy confuses workers about what their standards of living can be, they make estimates. These subjective judgments are based on how much money others appear to be making; how important, difficult, unpleasant, or dangerous various jobs are; trends of the national standard of living; and even such intangibles as what schools the employees attended.

That workers and consumers make demands that have little relation to what the economy can provide is therefore not surprising. If someone does not know how much economic pie his daily toil produces, the worker-capitalist class-struggle myth convinces him that his share is too small. Indeed, public-opinion surveys have shown that a majority of people think that they are underpaid; few believe that they are overpaid. Thus, Americans' conceptions of what they should earn represent considerably more consumer goods and services than the economy can produce.

Our economy was not always complex, and the value of work uncertain. The pioneer family knew what its efforts were worth. The size of the frontiersman's cabin, the number of bearskins on his rustic bed, and the quantity of rabbit stew and cornbread on his children's plates were closely related to how hard he and his wife worked.

In small towns, even when currency was used as a medium of exchange, people's labors were still readily identifiable with specific quantities of goods and services. The cooper, and probably many of his fellow villagers as well, knew how many barrels he could turn out in a month. And most people knew the worth of those barrels relative to sugar, horseshoes, and flour because they had a reasonably sound knowledge of the work that went into each product.

Knowing what effort produced a weekly newspaper, a set of horseshoes, or a sack of flour was not so difficult, partly because each of those items was made the same way year after year. Infrequent were the innovations that dramatically increased the blacksmith's or the printer's or other workers' output, and therefore lowered the cost of his products. Of course, farmers and fishermen experienced good and bad seasons that reduced or increased the value of a bushel of corn or a hundred pounds of cod. But generally the value of one product relative to another changed little.

The nineteenth century, which brought the Industrial Revolution, presented new circumstances. Technological progress rapidly raised the average person's capacity to produce and with it the American standard of living. Inventions—harvesters, locomotives, cotton gins, new production techniques, and numerous other advances—helped workers improve productivity. The economic pie grew faster than the nation's population.

Technological change accelerated in the twentieth century. In the post–World War II era, the relationship between a worker's efforts and his product changed often, continually in some industries. For example, the productivity of an airline pilot, measured in passenger-miles per hour (number of passengers in plane times miles per hour), increased dramatically between the end of the war and the early Seventies. A pilot of a Boeing Stratocruiser, the largest airliner of the 1940s, achieved a maximum of 30,000 passenger-miles per hour. In the Sixties, the captain of a Boeing 707 could fly about 105,000 passenger-miles per hour. And the pilot of the giant 747, which started service in the Seventies, could attain as many as 313,000 passenger-miles per hour—more than ten times the productivity of a quarter-century earlier.

As productivity rose, real prices of transportation, food, clothing, and other consumer goods and services fell at varying rates. A worker with average income could buy 2.3 times as many eggs in 1970 as in 1950 with the same portion of his after-tax wages. He could also purchase 1.6 times as much clothing for himself and his family, but only 1.1 times as much medical care. Keeping track of the relative values of goods and services was not always easy.

The new era brought increasing specialization, which obscured the value of work. Gone was the day when the blacksmith and the printer could each appreciate the time, effort, and talent his neighbor spent producing nails or newspapers. Today, one would be hard pressed to find an employee of the *New York Times* who knows how nails are made at Gunnison-International, Inc., or an employee of Gunnison who knows how many man-hours are required to put a newspaper on his doorstep every morning.

With progress has come change, growth, and increasing specialization. Our economy has become so complicated that a person can no longer evaluate his contribution to the economic pie. Nor can he compare his contribution to those of other workers. As a result, we are less sure of how to equitably distribute consumer purchasing power.

Labor markets are supposed to link workers' compensations to their contributions to the economic pie. However, obstacles to the proper operation of these markets have been growing. Some employees have won large pay increases relative to other workers without increasing their contributions to production. These employees have obtained more pie at the expense of other consumers.

Specialization and technological progress are largely responsible for changing the labor markets. These developments have raised the costs of recruiting, selecting, and training employees. When these costs, and not just the value of a worker's efforts, become important considerations in hiring, firing, and pay decisions, the efficiency of labor markets declines.

A century ago, a large proportion of jobs required little training and few skills. Muscle, stamina, and a willingness to perspire were the attributes of a good worker. Many of the people who labored in fields, in mines, at construction sites, and in mills were largely interchangeable. Job training was often a simple statement of duties: "Here's your shovel. Dig."

Today, in our highly specialized economy, most workers are not interchangeable. A person usually cannot dig unless he is skillful at operating complicated earthmoving equipment. To become a competent salesclerk, computer programmer, carpenter, mechanic, chemical engineer, chef, 747 pilot, advertising copywriter, microsurgeon, tax lawyer, or stereo serviceman, one must have weeks, months, years, or even decades of training and experience. A pilot is not about to switch to copywriting when air travel slumps.

Specialization enables many of today's employees to continue to win higher compensation, even when the state of the economy is poor and millions of men and women vainly hunt for jobs. The rate of unemployment may be high, but competent offset-printing press operators, electronic-typewriter-service personnel, bilingual teachers, piano tuners, and automobile-transmission mechanics, for instance, may be scarce. Their employers will pay dearly to keep them.

Employers' fears of losing valuable personnel have grown along with the costs of finding and training replacements. As occupations have become more specialized, the bargaining positions of many employees have strengthened. Today the director of a research laboratory may hesitate to dismiss a less than satisfactory technician despite the availability of bright replacements. He spent considerable time and effort to train this assistant; he does not want to duplicate his investment. A newcomer may have to become acquainted with the nature of complex research projects, unique computer software, and procedures peculiar to the laboratory.

While specialization slowly strengthened the bargaining positions of some employees vis-à-vis their employers, many workers discovered a dramatic way to increase their negotiating power. They organized unions. Workers became more successful at pursuing their aspirations for higher compensation and less work.

Wages and salaries in the United States remained fairly constant until the post–World War II era. From 1860 to 1950, hourly pay rose at an average rate of 2.8% annually. But from 1950 to 1970, the rate of pay increases averaged 4.5% annually. And from 1970 to 1980, the rise was 7.6%.

Prior to World War II, whenever the unemployment rate soared, wages were depressed. Nowadays, a serious economic slump can only slow the rate of pay increases. Specialization and unionization have made the bargaining positions of employees so strong that their efforts to obtain higher compensation are generally successful.

Even the downward pressure on pay that comes with a severe recession reduces wages only in scattered instances. Nothing less than a depression would halt the rise in the average wage.

The annual pay raise is an institution. Even workers who perform no better from one year to the next believe that periodic increases are rightfully theirs. Raises make people happy. They can bring enhanced self-worth, additional status, and, most of all, an instantly—if temporarily—higher standard of living. The experience of Americans during most of the post–World War II era taught them to look to pay increases for bigger shares of pie. But pay raises cannot improve the national standard of living; only increased production can do that.

The past hundred years, especially in the United States, were characterized by increases in productivity that were reflected in the standard of living. Although the annual gains in per-capita output were usually small, the differences in the standard of living from generation to generation were dramatic. As a result of higher productivity, people were able to work a shorter week and still enjoy more material comforts.

Children growing up at the turn of the century were fortunate if their parents owned a horse and buggy. If these youngsters, when they became adults, were able to maintain a favorable standard of living relative to the rest of the population, *their* children enjoyed riding in a Model T and took electric lights for granted. Twenty-five years later, airplanes carried the latest generation across the country to visit their grandparents. By 1980, a whole world of new products had become commonplace, including video games, home computers, telephone-answering machines, self-cleaning ovens, disposable diapers, air-conditioned automobiles, synthetic detergents, antibiotics, and automatic bank tellers.

The glorious advances in consumer products at the same time that pay scales were rising created the illusion that higher wages and salaries cause increases in real incomes. However, the simultaneous growth of both the economic pie and pay rates was mere coincidence. Pay increases cannot by themselves produce goods or services.

Had wages and salary rates stayed where they were, purchasing power would have risen anyway. The gains in productivity would then have led to lower dollar production costs and thus to lower prices. All of us are familiar with price decreases that stem from increases in productivity. The costs of electronic calculators, long-distance telephone calls, and air travel have all declined at various times in recent decades when technological progress increased efficiency.

Until the 1970s, American prosperity was not noticeably harmed or threatened by the common perception of a "class struggle" between business and its employees, and by the widespread failure to recognize the real struggle between consumers and workers. The consequences of the popular association of pay increases with bigger economic pies were also fairly benign.

Then the world began to change. Global scarcities of many basic materials from salmon to petroleum started to occur. As other nations became increasingly industrialized, international competition became keener, often reducing the relative desirability of American goods in world trade. Furthermore, some American productive energies had to be diverted to cleaning up and protecting the environment. The steady upward course of American productivity began to waver and hesitate. Toward the end of the Seventies, the standard of living stopped growing and began to shrink.

Although our society encountered difficulties in achieving gains in production, consumers suffered no loss of appetite for goods and services. The economy failed to support its constituents in the ever grander manner that they had come to expect. The consequent disappointment of consumers has been aggravating the hidden struggle between workers and consumers.

People had lost sight of that basic law, "Society cannot long consume more than it produces." In an effort to live the way they "have a right to," workers, be they unskilled factory hands or neurosurgeons, have continued to demand higher compensations. This situation, as we will see, had much more to do with the inflation of the 1970s—and 1980s—than anything government has done.

Americans can no longer afford to tolerate the Marxist myth. In

the face of the challenges of the decades ahead, the worker-capitalist class-struggle myth is a serious threat to the proper functioning
of the American economy. The pressures squeezing our standard of
living will increasingly aggravate the hidden struggles in our society
between worker and consumer, and among groups of consumers.
Unless we learn to recognize our genuine, basic, economic conflicts, and face the reality that the United States' pies in the 1980s
will not be as large as we had once hoped, we will not be able to
take measures that will increase employment and output, and limit
inflation.

By obscuring our real concerns, the Marxist myth allows selfish-
ness to masquerade as righteousness. In the name of the working
class, many employees demand and win raises that permit them to
unfairly obtain larger pieces of the economic pie. But millions of
consumers lose the battle for pie only because they possess little or
no power to raise their incomes. Their plight offends any reasonable
conception of justice.

Unfair slicing of the pie is only half of the cost to society of
clinging to the myth of a business-worker contest based on wage
rates. Americans' misunderstanding severely hinders output by promoting counterproductive behavior.

In most firms, a conflict between the boss and his subordinates
does exist. The boss wishes that those reporting to him would work
harder and that he could pay them less. They have another idea:
They want to be paid more and work fewer hours. *Nonetheless the
interests of both employer and employee are served when their opposing objectives do not interfere with the smooth functioning of the
enterprise.* So are the interests of all American consumers.

Conflicts over working hours, compensation, and other job conditions often stir animosities that reduce efficiency. Employees,
whether they are individuals, unorganized groups, or union members, may harbor harsh feelings toward their management, whom
they see as surrogate owners. These workers often lose interest in
their jobs, do only what is required and no more. They may not
bother to report a machine that needs maintenance. Unconcerned
employees may allow questionable market research to become the

basis for a sales campaign. Assemblers may install parts that they know are faulty.

As myth would have it, even bosses who are employees themselves are the workers' enemies. They represent the company, and therefore its owners. They give orders and sometimes grant raises. Therefore, middle managers often have dual roles; sometimes they are employees struggling against their employers, and sometimes they are managers struggling against their subordinates. A rank-and-file worker who is promoted to foreman is no longer entirely on the employee side of the employee-employer struggle.

The most destructive battles between employers and employees are strikes and lockouts. The amount of time lost through work stoppages may appear to be barely significant until one looks at the repercussions. A strike by relatively few people can halt the activities of a great many other workers. Such a stoppage can noticeably reduce the size of the economic pie by disrupting "bystanders"—enterprises that depend on the shut-down organization for materials. Deprived of necessary parts or services, they may have to curtail their own operations.

For example, an autumn 1970 strike closed General Motors' American plants. As a consequence, production was reduced and workers were laid off at tire, glass, steel, copper, and many other manufacturers that depended on GM's patronage. Dealers and their salesmen lost income. Retail stores whose customers included employees of General Motors and its suppliers also suffered financially. Indeed, the lingering of the 1969–70 recession was partly attributable to the GM–United Auto Workers dispute.

Among the strikes that have the most extensive ill effects are those that tie up transportation. When trucks, railroads, or municipal bus lines cease operations, the losses inflicted upon businesses and individuals are often widespread and severe. A number of cities have been staggered in recent years by strikes that paralyzed their transit systems.

To illustrate, in 1980 the New York City transit workers' strike involved 33,000 workers, but it deprived millions of people of their usual means of traveling to work, school, stores, and so forth. A quarter of a million of them were unable to reach their jobs at all. Many tourists and out-of-town business people were discouraged from traveling to New York. The city's 22 largest department stores suffered sales declines of from 30% to 35%. Five thousand companies had to resort to low-interest loans from the Small Business Administration in order to protect their solvency. Firms and workers alike incurred losses that aggregated far more than the amount that the city and the union were quarreling over.

A strike need not involve thousands of people to interfere with the smooth operation of the economy. In this age of growing reliance on computers, sophisticated communications apparatus, and other electric wizardry, the men and women who operate this equipment often wield vast power. During the 1981 strike of the American air-traffic controllers, the sympathetic job action of a handful of their colleagues in Newfoundland that lasted a few days resulted in the cancellation or delay of most transatlantic flights. Thousands of people were stranded an ocean away from their destinations.

The class-struggle myth increases the likelihood that the natural conflicts of interest between individual workers and bosses will grow into animosity that overshadows their common interests. The myth can magnify worker grievances and escalate disagreements with management to, in the employee's eyes, romantic episodes in a universal struggle of the underclass against oppression. Workers who believe they are unfairly treated may take actions against the company that have an aura of righteousness. Such actions range from cutting corners to, in extreme cases, vandalism or other violence. The myth can induce otherwise responsible citizens to slash tires and overturn vehicles—and feel that they have performed heroic acts!

Worker-boss tension can arise quite easily without widespread acceptance of a class struggle, but against the background of the Marxist myth, it is likely to be exacerbated. A number of causes may aggravate the inevitable differences between employee and superior to produce hostility and counterproductive behavior. Managements may be inconsiderate or neglectful of employee concerns. Superiors may be incompetent. Unions may assume militant, adversary roles that encourage managements to look upon their employees with disdain.

Even government workers, who cannot complain that their employers are exploiting them for profit, are not uncommonly angry at their bosses. Employees of the state in Poland, Russia, Britain, and America can be and often are disgruntled. They may believe that their superiors are unreasonable, stupid, unfair, and generally incompetent. But they cannot claim that their bosses are cheating them by taking unconscionable profits.

Marx asserted that the capitalist's profit really belonged to his employees. Even if management was considerate and competent, it would still be exploiting the workers. A great many people who do not think of themselves as Marxists believe that workers and managements are inexorably locked into a contest in which the former are trying to limit the extent to which the latter take advantage of them. The class-struggle myth gives employers and employees a philosophical basis for dividing themselves into opposing camps. Harmony and cooperation are bound to suffer. The myth provides a rationale for management-employee friction.

To say that worker-management cooperation can be better is not an overly idealistic statement. It has been demonstrated not only by individual firms but by an entire nation.

The myth of a class struggle between workers and the owners of business is much stronger in Great Britain than in the United States, yet it is barely present in Japan. This distinction is perhaps the most important reason why the British economy is a shambles while Japanese achievements are inspiring worldwide admiration, even awe.

The two countries have major cultural differences, of course, but they also have a number of striking similarities. Each is an island nation with a long history. Each evolved from a feudal society into a democratic kingdom. Each has a racially and religiously homogeneous population, strong traditions, and national pride. Both countries were severely battered during the Second World War. Japan had to rebuild with virtually no resources except, as many Japanese proudly state, its people. Britain has important raw materials, including coal, oil, and natural gas. It also has a long history of invention and technological accomplishment. The Industrial Revolution began there. Britain has given the world many of its greatest scientists, political philosophers, and writers. Japan was late to emerge from feudalism and enter the age of industrialization. Although the Japanese tradition is also rich, it has not until recently encompassed technological progress.

In view of these observations, the remarkable differences between these nations' current economic health might seem puzzling. However, not if we look at some of the differences in their social ideologies.

The British are particularly susceptible to myths about class struggles because of their long tradition of class distinction. Not only economic status, but accents, schools, and ancestry continue to keep Englishmen apart from one another. In this environment, workers are considerably influenced by ideologies that assert that the proletariat's interests are in conflict with capitalists. Employers are eyed with suspicion. The Marxist myth thrives.

Labor in the United Kingdom fights well for its ideology. Its achievements—featherbedding, resistance to technological advances, and cumbersome work rules—are so extraordinary that one can easily overlook the millions of Britons who work as hard and diligently as people anywhere else. Still, many British workers have succeeded in doing less work and in working less efficiently than their counterparts in other industrialized nations. Their victory is an important reason for their nation's relatively small gains in per-capita gross national product. From 1959 to 1979, per-capita real GNP in the United Kingdom advanced at an average annual rate of 2.3%. Japan's progress was outstanding, a gain of 7.5% a year. Standing between Japan and the United Kingdom were other European nations that in 1959 were comparable to Britain in productivity and standard of living. Germany had an average annual improvement in product per capita of 3.5%; Italy 3.7%; France and Austria 4.0%. (The United States fared relatively poorly with 2.4%, but it started from a much higher level than the other nations, including the United Kingdom.)

That the British labor force performs far below capacity was demonstrated in 1974. Because a lengthy coal miners' strike threatened to completely throttle the economy, the government ordered most industries to shorten the workweek to three days in order to conserve fuel. Either the exhilaration of four-day weekends had a fantastic, vitalizing effect on British workers, or they had been producing at a rate far below their ability. Although hours were reduced 40%, output fell only 15%. Workers suddenly increased their productivity 27%!

The "gains" of labor in the United Kingdom have often been abetted by poor or indifferent managements. Aloof executives fail to take advantage of workers' knowledge and experience. Indeed, they are prone to be unmindful—sometimes disdainful—of their employees' needs and aspirations. Moreover, their leadership may not inspire hard work. If some British executives observe tradition, they take Thursday-to-Monday weekends and do not deign to be at their desks before 9:30 in the morning.

The workers have won great concessions in what they believe is a class struggle against capitalists, but they have not succeeded in raising their standard of living to desired levels. The reason: their struggle has really been against all their nation's consumers, including themselves. They have produced too little economic pie. The British have the lowest standard of living among the major industrial peoples of Western Europe. Moreover, their relative position has been slipping over the long term.

On the other hand, Japan, a late arrival among the technologically advanced powers, was regarded not long ago as the habitat of lame industrial copycats. But in 1980 Japan became the leading producer of automobiles. It has the most efficient steel capacity in the world, and one of the largest. An American easily has the impression, which is almost accurate, that all cameras, stereo components, and calculators come from Japan.

A reason for Japan's success is that almost nobody pays attention to a class-struggle myth. Certainly an educated population, intelligent planning, and a cooperative government share much of the credit for the Japanese achievement. But perhaps most important is the way in which business and its employees identify their interests with one another. Management and workers join hands to meet the challenges of keen competition at home and in the markets of the world. Productivity is high and strikes are relatively rare.

Japanese employers and employees often make what amounts to a lifetime commitment to each other. Many people work for only one company from graduation day to retirement. In exchange for his loyalty, the worker is offered not only job security but extensive training, comprehensive economic benefits for himself and his family, and the feeling that he is a part of the organization whether times are good or poor. Companies train personnel without fear of losing their investment through employee turnover. They therefore have a reservoir of able, experienced people at all times.

Managers and workers have excellent communication. Employees are informed of goals and progress. A worker knows why he is performing the tasks he has been assigned, why they are important, and how his performance will be evaluated. Managers frequently appear on the production floor and in the offices of subordinates to exchange ideas, give encouragement, and direct activities. Workers often participate in making the decisions that affect them.

Labor-management cooperation directed toward improving productivity has transformed Japan from a defeated, somewhat underdeveloped country at the end of World War II to the envy of the industrial world. An ethic of work prevails among workers, be they executives or those who work at the more menial jobs. Subordinates and their bosses strive to assure that work stoppages and poor productivity are avoided. As a result, Japanese consumers are not the victims of a struggle with Japanese workers. Quite the contrary.

The Japanese remind us of the importance of focusing on the purpose of the economy: to produce and distribute consumer goods and services. Like them, we should remember that, over the long run, consumption is limited by production. And we should emulate their emphasis on cooperation among workers—be their tasks menial or managerial—as a means of promoting productivity.

Many successful American firms *have* achieved high degrees of teamwork among their personnel—even long before Japan became a world economic power. However, many Americans—managers, stockholders, union members, nonunion workers, politicians, and academics—believe that employment represents a truce, often an uneasy one, between two parties with inherently conflicting goals, parties that do not have a common objective.

The Japanese system is not perfect. Questions about its viability over a lengthy period will be answered only with the passage of time. Moreover, Japanese society lacks the great emphasis on the individual that is so profound a part of American history, tradition, and everyday life. Our business practices cannot be improved without regard to our culture. Nevertheless, we would do well to emulate the Japanese devotion to worker-boss cooperation.

Lest we overemphasize the role of culture in business, we must remember that Japan has been basking in prosperity during the postwar period. Times were never so bad and competition so tough that managements were forced to shift priorities from the achievement of long-term success to assuring survival in the short run. Neither inflation nor OPEC has been allowed by the government to slow the economy much or for long. Japan has enjoyed ample profits, growth, and full employment almost continuously. Business has been financially able to undertake expensive obligations to its employees and fulfill them. It has been able to provide job security and make long-term investments in training and in plant and equipment.

In any country, when adverse economic conditions reduce sales, attitudes harden. Managements demand more efficiency in order to attain at least some profits. Employees, fearful of losing their jobs, may become more productive. But sometimes they will slow their efforts in order to prolong the work. In the United States, featherbedding and many of the rules that interfere with the efficient deployment of manpower and the use of new machines and techniques were the results of employees seeking means to preserve their jobs during bad times.

A company struggling to survive certainly has difficulty being considerate to its employees. As it scrimps on wages, paper towels in the rest rooms, and food in the cafeteria, it begins to annoy, anger, and frighten its workers. A marginal business is unlikely to have exemplary relations with its personnel. Indeed, such a company and its employees tend to see each other as necessary evils to be endured but not deserving of any gratuitous consideration. Hard times exacerbate whatever antagonisms already exist.

What the American economy needs is, first of all, a recognition of the identity of interests between investors and workers—of those who benefit from profits and those who depend on wages and salaries. The myth that profits represent exploitation must be laid to rest. We also need economic policies that consistently assure enough profits and full employment. They would do more than put an end to the unemployment problem; they would create an atmosphere of stability and confidence. Then firms would be more likely to improve their relations with their employees, more people would be contributing to the economic pie, and productivity would be higher.

The consequences of the Marxist class-struggle myth are not serious during periods of rapid growth in the standard of living. However, when the standard of living is threatened, as it will continue to be for at least the next decade, the costs of the myth are severe. America had better open its eyes.

In some ways, American business is awakening to the need to reassess our traditional views of the employee-employer relationship. New approaches to human-resource management have been tried by some firms with success. Workers have been consulted on new plant designs. Greater efforts have been made, when jobs have become obsolete, to train employees for other tasks within the same company. More credit is being given and attention paid to those corporations that have especially imaginative and successful labor relations. And, significantly, American managers are scrutinizing Japanese methods.

The United States is a nation of people who are not disposed to dragging their feet when change is needed. Hopefully we will move away from the Marxist myth. Our chances will increase if the government can improve business conditions and raise employment.

Prosperity depends on one essential element of our economy. We must again turn our attention to profits.

# 4

# The Sources of Profits

Where do profits come from? Everyone knows that firms obtain profits because their revenues exceed their expenses. But if all business keeps taking in more than it pays out, where in the economy does the excess originate? Few people ponder this question although we live in a profit-driven economy. When individuals do volunteer answers, they are usually vague and almost invariably wrong.

Yet an incontrovertible explanation of how the economy generates profits does exist. Profits flow from several sources, each of which is a clearly identifiable economic phenomenon. The variations in these flows determine the profitability of American business—whether it experiences prosperity, recession, or something in between.

Popular notions about where business's profits come from have little relationship to reality. The variety of language Americans use to describe the act of securing profits reflects their confusion; a single individual might say all of the following in the course of a day: "We *made* a profit." "International Oil Ltd. *ripped off* consumers for a huge profit." And, "General Products Corporation *earned* $4.11 a share."

Obviously, there is more to the generation of profits than the creativity, greediness, or merit of business. The combined effort of all American enterprises to obtain profits changes gradually, if at all, yet the total amount of U.S. profits often swings erratically from year to year, even from quarter to quarter. No lapse in business's exertions can explain why corporate profits fell from $10 billion in 1929 to $3.7 billion in 1930, and to $ −0.4 billion and $ −2.3 billion in the next two years. Nor can any manic-depressive behavior of business people explain why profits have dropped at least 20% during every post–World War II recession and then usually recovered rapidly.

Dips in total profits occur despite the energetic, even heroic, efforts of individual firms. During the worst periods of the Great Depression, most companies reacted by striving harder to deliver good products efficiently. Yet salesmen experienced unaccustomed difficulty in filling their order books, and cash registers rang infrequently. During any slump, firms take unusual pains to improve their profitability by cutting costs, intensifying sales efforts, and offering extra services.

The sources of profits will show us why, throughout history, business has not been able to control the nation's aggregate profitability, but has instead been the victim or beneficiary of the variable economic climate. Like schoolchildren competing for prizes, firms cannot determine how large the awards will be; each one can only do its best to win as many of the prizes that are offered as it possibly can.

Most twentieth-century economists have viewed these fluctuations in profits as little more than symptoms of the business cycle. They have therefore devoted their researches to other concerns, all but ignoring the question "Where do profits come from?" But fluctuations in total profits are critical. In our profit-motivated economy, the sources of profits are the key to understanding changes in production, employment, and investment—in the overall economic climate.

Of course, economists have studied some aspects of profits. Theoreticians have explored such issues as why *individual* firms secure profits, what services investors render in return for profits, and whether profits are justified. Their theories variously assert that profits are premiums earned by investors for bearing risks, results of monopoly power, rewards for innovation, and so forth. However, few of these ideas even begin to explain where in the economy the flows of money that become profits originate.

Of the best-known economists, the one who may have looked most deeply into how profits arise was, ironically, not a supporter of free enterprise, but Karl Marx. He attributed profits to capitalists taking "surplus value" from the proletariat by paying them less than the value of the work they performed. Robert Heilbroner, a gifted writer and distinguished economist, discusses this theory at length in his book *Marxism: For and Against.* Heilbroner appears favorably disposed to the concept of surplus value, but concedes that it is "unprovable" and "heuristic." He adds that "the theory of surplus value provides an explanation for a problem that has always been the Achilles heel of economics, namely, the sources of profits. Unwilling to attribute profits to the transfer of wealth from one class to another, bourgeois economists have struggled in vain to explain profits."

The sources of profits have been overlooked for so long that you would think they must be well hidden. Not so. They are thinly concealed in one of the best-known relationships in economics: "saving = investment." This equation is valid because of the ways in which "saving" and "investment" are defined, as John Maynard Keynes explained in his famous book *The General Theory of Employment, Interest, and Money.* Moreover, finding the sources of profits by means of this law of economics does not rely on any theories or assumptions.

To see how Lord Keynes reached his conclusion, we start with saving. What is saving? Your own saving is your income minus the amount that you spend. If your after-tax income is $1,000 and you use $800 for food, clothing, and all your other purchases, you save $200. The nation's total saving is essentially the same. Whether we are referring to one person or the whole economy:

$$\text{Saving} = \text{Income} - \text{Consumption.}$$

And investment? Most output is for consumption and is represented metaphorically by the "economic pie." The rest of the economy's production is investment. It includes such products as factory buildings, bulldozers, office computers, and railroad track. These goods and other kinds of investment are not part of the present pie, but they will contribute to the economy's ability to produce consumer goods and services in the future. So investment is current output that is not currently consumed. Thus:

$$\text{Investment} = \text{Output} - \text{Consumption}.$$

We need one more piece of the puzzle before we can put it all together and have the saving-investment equation. The missing piece is the fact that income and output are equal. Think of our old friend Robinson Crusoe. His income certainly *was* his output. Even though the American economy is far larger and more complex than Crusoe's, our nation's income is its output. This principle holds true in any economy:

$$\text{Income} = \text{Output}.$$

Therefore:

$$\text{Income} - \text{Consumption} = \text{Output} - \text{Consumption}.$$

We already know that income − consumption is saving, and output − consumption is investment. Therefore,

$$\text{Saving} = \text{Investment}.$$

In our everyday lives, we often talk about saving and investment in the same breath:

"Joe, I've saved two thousand dollars."

"What are you going to do with that money, Fred?"

"I don't know, Joe. I'm thinking of investing it in my brother-in-law's new restaurant or in AT&T bonds."

Whether Fred puts his money into his brother-in-law's venture or into AT&T, we see that saving and investment are indeed two sides of the same coin. In one case, the money that Fred saves is invested in ranges, utensils, and other restaurant equipment. In the other, it may finance the purchase of a computerized switchboard.

Saving was equal to investment long before we had bond markets and other financial institutions. Here is part of an ancient story about saving and investment.

Then Joseph said to Pharaoh, "The dream of Pharaoh is one; God has revealed to Pharaoh what he is about to do. . . . There will come seven years of great plenty throughout all the land of Egypt, but after them there will arise seven years of famine, and all the plenty will be forgotten in the land of Egypt. . . . Let Pharaoh proceed to appoint over-seers over the land, and take the fifth part of the produce of the land of Egypt during the seven plenteous years. And let them gather all the food of these good years that are coming, and lay up grain under the authority of Pharaoh for food in the cities, and let them keep it. That food shall be a reserve for the land against the seven years of famine which are to befall the land of Egypt, so that the land may not perish through the famine." (Genesis 41:25–36)

The grain that the ancient Egyptians saved was an investment in their future.

Saving and investment are equal in any era, in any country. Any economist is aware of this relationship and would be no more likely to doubt it than a mathematician would be to challenge the statement "$4 + 4 = 8$."

Most people, when they think of saving, envision individuals depositing money in a bank, mailing a check to a money-market fund, or conducting a similar transaction. But individuals are not the only savers. Governments save when their receipts are larger than their outlays. Although the federal government has been a profligate in recent years, state and local jurisdictions have generally recorded surpluses—that is, savings.

Another category of savers is comprised of corporations. Some of their saving is called "undistributed profits"—that is, profits that are retained and not paid to the government as income taxes or to shareholders as dividends. We are especially interested in undistributed profits. The rest of business saving is other money that is retained—it is designated (in official statistics) "capital consumption allowances." (This money is not part of profits because it covers a cost—primarily the depreciation of business's structures, equipment, and so forth.)

We emphasize that these terms and relationships are not our own inventions, but widely used and accepted. The United States Department of Commerce regularly publishes a table called "Saving and Investment Account," a statement of saving = investment. Fig.

1 represents that table. (Note: As a matter of convenience, we omit one of the table's items, which usually equals zero and is never significant. It is called "wage accruals less disbursements.")

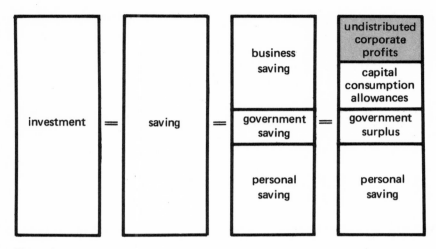

Figure 1

By rearranging the parts of Fig. 1, we can see that undistributed corporate profits equal investment *minus* the sum of capital consumption, government saving, and personal saving, as shown in Fig. 2.

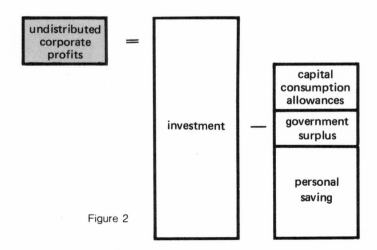

Figure 2

So far we have split saving into four parts. In order to help identify the sources of profits, we also divide investment into three parts: fixed investment, change in business inventories, and net foreign investment. (These terms, which are used by the Department of Commerce in its national accounts tables, will be explained more fully later. For now, it is sufficient to recognize that each is a particular category of investment.) Now our diagram appears as shown in Fig. 3.

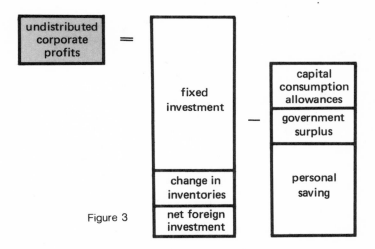

Figure 3

We take one more step. Undistributed profits are profits left after corporate income taxes have been paid to the government and dividends have been distributed to shareholders. Thus the diagram shown in Fig. 4.

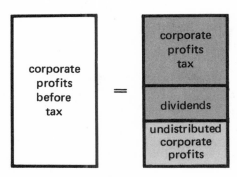

Figure 4

Adding dividends and corporate-profits tax on each side of the equals sign in Fig. 3, we obtain the diagram shown in Fig. 5.

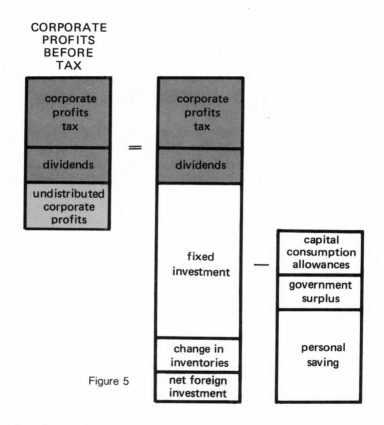

Figure 5

Voila! The sources of profits:

$$
\text{corporate profits before tax} \quad = \quad
\begin{array}{l}
\text{+ fixed investment} \\
\text{+ change in business inventories} \\
\text{+ net foreign investment} \\
\text{− personal saving} \\
\text{− capital consumption allowances} \\
\text{− government surplus (or + deficit)} \\
\text{+ dividends} \\
\text{+ corporate profits tax}
\end{array}
$$

You may wonder why we have not included the profits of unin-corporated business enterprises. The reason is that neither we nor anyone else can definitively say what they are. Do unincorporated farmers, for example, secure profits? No one knows, because the accounting practices of noncorporate businesses do not specify how much of their income is wages earned by the owners and how much is profits. If farmers and other entrepreneurs paid themselves reasonable wages, would their enterprises show any profits? No one can be certain. By not designating any of the income of nonincorporated enterprises as profits, we are conforming to the convention used by the Department of Commerce, the Department of Labor, the Internal Revenue Service, and other agencies.

At first glance, one may not be convinced that this equation is particularly profound or useful. After all, what does it prove except that corporate profits are always equal to the sum of the terms on the right-hand side of the equals sign? As we examine them more closely, their relationships to profits will become evident.

Exploring the equation's implications, we will reach numerous conclusions about how our system works that are crucial and often surprising. Already the equation tells us some interesting things. Suppose, for example, that fixed investment increased by $10 billion, while all of the other profit sources remained as they were. The equation says profits must also rise by $10 billion; it suggests that a rise in fixed investment increases business profitability.

On the other hand, one might look at the equation and conclude that if *profits* increase, investment—or other terms on the right— must change. The equation does not imply anything about causality—which items are causes and which others are effects.

Another aspect of this equation may be puzzling: Some of its implications seem to run counter to common experience. For example, investors know that dividends tend to rise as a result of higher profits, but dividends appear as a profit source. "How on earth can dividends increase profits?" one may wonder. We will see how dividends and even profits taxes paid by corporations circulate in the economy and become part of the flow of money that returns to business to become profits anew.

In essence, what is still missing is an explanation of how the items we call "profit sources" affect profits. So far we have shown that profits must be equal to a list of economic quantities. Our proof, the application of some simple math to an incontrovertible statement, is as sound as any ever offered in mathematics or physics. But neither the equation nor the way we derived it explains a process by which the terms on the right-hand side of the equals sign create profits.

The equation of the sources of profits *does* represent a process, one that is as fundamental to an economy as respiration is to a living organism. A comprehension of this process enables us to understand our system and cope with its problems. In this chapter, we have seen only a static picture. But our economy is a dynamic system. In the next chapter, we will look at the economy in motion. We will see *how* it works, how profits are generated.

# 5

## The Economy in Motion

Money flows through the economy like blood through a human being or water through an intricate network of pipes. Wages, profits, sales, taxes, and dividends are all *flows* of money, not static sums that sit in bank accounts or treasuries.

For example, a worker's annual salary may be $15,000 after taxes, but he may never have as much as $1,000 at any time during the year. He receives his income in weekly installments of $300. Meanwhile, he continually uses this money for a number of purposes—to buy food, pay the electric bill, purchase clothing, and so forth. Thus, the dollars that he earns flow on through the system, playing many additional roles. The economy is dynamic. The money the worker spends at the grocery store becomes revenue to the proprietor, then revenue to Campbell's Soup, then wages for a Campbell employee, and so on.

People often compare wages and profits as if they were slices of the same pie. But because our economy is dynamic, the pie analogy, which was so appropriate for discussing consumer goods and services, is inadequate for describing the relationship between wages and profits. A sandwich, a shirt, or a shoeshine is generally consumed by one person, so each is reasonably represented by a piece of pie. A dollar, on the other hand, circulates continually; it may be received and spent by many different individuals and organizations over the course of a year. Since profits and wages are flows of money, any model that represents them must reflect the circulation of dollars.

51

We therefore choose to view the economy as a network of pipes through which money flows like water. This analogy will help identify the particular flows that bring profits to business. We will represent each kind of payment, transfer, or other transaction that affects profits with a specific pipe.

Our society has too many people, corporations, and even government units for us to look at each one individually, so we organize them into categories called "sectors." With sectors we can discuss *total* consumer saving, *total* business purchases of plant and equipment, or *total* government tax receipts. These aggregations enable us to think, for example, of a single pipe through which wages and salaries flow from businesses to their employees. Otherwise we would have to keep track of 80 million separate tubes, one for each employee.

For our purpose—to trace the flows of money that wind up as profits—we divide the economy into five sectors: household, government, foreign, consumer goods, and capital goods. The last two are sometimes referred to together as the business sector.

*The household sector* is all of us Americans in our roles as consumers. It also includes not-for-profit organizations, such as churches and private schools, which are conventionally viewed as groups of individual consumers. Wages, dividends, and other kinds of income flow into the household sector. Expenditures for goods and services and payments of taxes flow out. This sector is one we are all intimately familiar with.

*The government sector* comprises the federal and the thousands of state and local governments. The major pipelines to this sector are, of course, those that carry taxes in and those that take expenditures out. We will see what happens to profits when the inflow and outflow are not equal.

*The foreign sector* is not really part of our country's economy. It is the rest of the world—people, firms, governments, and other organizations that are located beyond the United States' boundaries. However, it is included as a sector because it is a source and a destination of money flows. Money that leaves our country goes through a pipe to the foreign sector. And money that flows into the United

States from abroad comes in a pipe from that sector.

*The business sector* consists of all the business enterprises, large and small, in the economy, viewed as if they were one huge conglomerate. Its profits are the profits and losses of all its individual enterprises added together. If a tiny economy had only four companies in its business sector and their respective profits were $8, $10, $12, and a loss of $5, the sector's profits would equal the sum, $25.

We divide the business sector into the capital-goods sector and the consumer-goods sector. Our plan is to find the sources of profits for each one separately. This process enables us to observe important characteristics of our economic system that would not otherwise be apparent. When we combine the two lists of profit sources, we will obtain the same result we achieved in chapter 4—that is, the same profit sources listed on page 48. But before we can discuss the consumer- and capital-goods sectors, we must define capital goods, consumer goods, and inventory goods.

*Capital goods* are durable goods used to produce other goods: lathes, factory buildings, railroad freight cars, bulldozers, and so forth. They have three important properties:

1. They are finished products (as opposed to parts or partially completed goods).

2. They are purchased by private enterprises (not by consumers or governments).

3. They have useful lives of more than one year and are depreciated over their lifetimes.

Depreciation is a process by which businesses recognize that capital goods gradually lose their value as they get older. Lathes, freight cars, and so forth are not used up rapidly like fuel, pencils, detergents, and typewriter ribbons. They will still be worth something a year or more after they are first put to work.

A plant manager would not say, "We had unusually high expenses this year; we spent fifty thousand dollars on a new truck. We should have it for five years at least; it's a solid piece of machinery."

Such a statement would be unrealistic because the truck should not be charged as an expense of a single year. A year after its purchase, its value would be, say, $40,000. The company's expense for the first year would be $10,000, not $50,000. It should not feel impoverished just because $40,000 of its holdings will no longer be in cash but in another kind of property.

In order to keep realistic books, firms *depreciate* their capital goods over their expected lifetimes. This means two things:

1. Firms do not consider the purchase of a capital good as an expense, but rather as a shift of their holdings from cash to physical property (in the same way that you would consider purchasing a bond or putting paper money in a bank savings account as an act of shifting your wealth from cash to another form of property).

2. Each year they indicate in their books that the capital good is worth less than it was the year before. They treat the resulting decrease in the value of their holdings as an expense of doing business. In the example above, the truck might be depreciated the same amount each year, $10,000, for each of the five years it is used. Only after the fifth year would the truck be worth zero dollars and be completely "used up."

This book is certainly not about accounting, so why make such a point about capital goods? Because we will have to understand what business expenses are in order to determine the sources of profits. Therefore, we must be aware that depreciation is an expense, but that purchases of capital goods are not.

*Consumer goods* are easy to define: all finished goods and services that are sold to individuals or governments—pork chops, television sets, haircuts, merry-go-round rides, sport coupes, sneakers, and so on. All government purchases—including school desks, telephone service, aircraft carriers, and red tape—are consumer goods. For convenience, we use the term "consumer goods" to refer to both goods and services.

Goods commonly bought by consumers are not classified as consumer goods if they are bought by business. For example, a copy of *Sports Illustrated* that a football fan buys at a newsstand is a consumer good, but a copy of the same magazine purchased by a corporation for the reception area of its headquarters is not a consumer good but an inventory good, defined below.

All other goods are *inventory goods*. They are parts, fuel, raw materials, supplies, and finished but unsold goods held by the business sector. Some examples are crude petroleum in Texaco's storage tanks, steel bars and plates at the Caterpillar tractor factory, new cars at the Chevrolet assembly plant, Heinz's beans on a supermarket's shelf, and soap for the lavatories of H & R Block's local office. Inventory goods are all goods owned by business that will be transformed, assembled, used up, or moved along to their ultimate user.

The three categories of goods—consumer, capital, and inventory—are all products of the business sector. The first two are produced respectively by the consumer-goods sector and the capital-goods sector. Each supplies itself with inventory goods.

*The capital-goods sector* includes not only the companies that produce finished capital goods but also all those that contribute to their manufacture. For example, Caterpillar Tractor Company is a manufacturer of bulldozers and other heavy equipment. These machines are capital goods; they are used by business and have lifetimes of more than one year. Therefore Caterpillar is part of the capital-goods sector. But so are the trucking firm that delivers its steel, the company that makes the steel, and the coal mine that sells fuel for the blast furnaces. To be part of the capital-goods sector, a firm has only to produce inventory goods or a service needed by the sector.

The capital-goods sector is largely self-contained. It does not buy anything from domestic firms that are not part of it. But it buys raw materials, parts, services, and even other capital goods from foreign countries.

*The consumer-goods sector* produces consumer goods and services, everything that the capital-goods sector does not produce. Like the capital-goods sector, it is largely self-contained. It, too, imports to fill some of its needs, but does not buy any services or inventory goods from domestic firms that are not part of it. However, it *does* purchase capital goods for its own use from the capital-goods sector.

Many firms serve two sectors. Suppose a steel company sells 40% of its output to Caterpillar, part of the capital-goods sector, and 60% of its steel to Maytag, a consumer-goods-sector enterprise. We would say that 40% of that steel company is in the capital-goods sector and 60% is in the consumer-goods sector. However, we do not need to concern ourselves with these fine distinctions. That we can conceptually separate the two sectors helps us to gain insights into the working of the economy and the generation of profits.

We are not interested in transactions among members of a sector. We are only concerned with flows of money that affect the overall position of the sector. To illustrate, think of a furniture factory. When it sells chairs to a retail store, it has revenue of, say, $5,000. This transaction does not affect the consumer-goods sector. The sector has increased neither its holdings of cash nor its inventory of chairs. It has merely shifted its assets—chairs and money—around within itself.

Only when a firm incurs an expense that is not recaptured by another enterprise in the same sector does the sector have an expense. Only when one sector sells a product to another sector does it have revenue. For instance, when the furniture store sells a chair to a consumer, the consumer-goods sector has revenue. And when the factory pays wages to an employee, the consumer-goods sector has an expense.

So we will regard the consumer-goods sector and the capital-goods sector as if each is one big company that supplies itself with all its own parts, raw materials, rented space, and so forth, except for what it buys from abroad. As we return to our pipeline analogy, we will only have to envision pipes carrying money to and from the sectors, not between organizations or individuals within a sector.

The definition of profits that appears at the beginning of this book is an accounting definition, commonly used by business, government, and virtually everyone else concerned with profits: profits are the excess of business revenues over business expenses. We will be elaborating on exactly what the revenue and expenses of the consumer-goods and capital-goods sectors are, using concepts generally accepted by private and governmental accountants as well as business people.*

---

* Notes and comments on the methods used in this analysis are at the end of the book (see pages 210–211). The notes identify and discuss simplifications made in the text (regarding interest expenses, for example) which do not affect our final result, the profit sources of the entire business sector.

The economic data used in this book were the latest available as it was being completed. Many of these statistics are subject to revision. The data in this chapter are scheduled to be revised by the Department of Commerce at least twice. The revisions will not in the least affect the points that we are making.

## THE PROFITS OF THE CONSUMER-GOODS SECTOR

Imagine all the revenue of the consumer-goods sector coming in through one pipe, and all its expenses running out through another. If the flows in these two pipes are equal, there is no profit or loss. In this case, the consumer-goods sector is merely a conduit: what comes in goes out (see Fig. 6).

However, if the inflows exceed the outflows, as they generally do, there is profit. The difference flows through the "profit pipeline" (Fig. 7) and adds to the sector's net worth. If expenses are greater than revenue, there is a net loss, and the flow through the profit pipeline is in the opposite direction, reducing the sector's net worth.

Profits, then, are whatever flows through the profit pipeline from right to left in Fig. 7. However, we cannot measure profits by simply checking the volume in the net worth storage tank. Why not? First, because the tank also holds money that stockholders have invested. Second, profits, once they have been obtained, do not necessarily remain in the firms that have collected them. Some are paid to investors as dividends. Others are paid to the government sector as corporate income taxes. Profits, like other kinds of income, are recirculated through the economy. Therefore, we will measure profits with a "profit meter" on the profit pipeline, an instrument comparable to the water meter that measures the use of water in a home.

Now we can begin to trace profits to their sources. To do so, we will look at the transactions in the economy that affect either consumer-goods-sector expenses or revenue. (Notice that this does *not* mean that we will consider every *type* of transaction in the economy; many have no effects whatsoever on revenues or expenses. For example, when a consumer sells a stock and buys a government bond, the transactions do not affect consumer-goods-sector expenses or revenues.)

At the outset, suppose our economy were very simple, with only the household and the consumer-goods sectors. Furthermore, suppose that the only income consumers had was the wages paid to them by the companies of the consumer-goods sector. Let's see what would have happened to profits in, for instance, 1980.

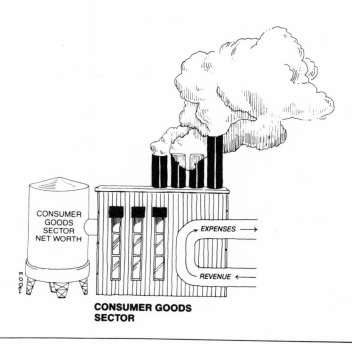

Figure 6. If revenue equals expenses, the consumer-goods sector has neither profit nor loss; the sector is merely a conduit: What comes in goes out.

Figure 7. If revenue exceeds expenses, the difference flows through the "profit pipeline," registers on the "profit meter," and adds to the sector's net worth.

The consumer-goods industry paid approximately $1,000 billion in wages and salaries during 1980—an immense amount. Nevertheless, even if consumers had spent every bit of this money, without saving so much as a cent, the consumer-goods sector would have received back only $1,000 billion, an amount that equaled its payroll costs. Since its receipts would have just equaled expenditures, it could not have secured a profit. Figure 8 illustrates this circular flow of money. For the consumer-goods sector to secure a profit on its payroll expenditures, its customers must have purchasing power that comes from sources other than the wages it pays them.

So how does the consumer-goods sector obtain a profit? The answer to the question is not affected by how high or low its wages are. *If businesses can only recover their wage and salary costs, no matter what the pay scale, the question still stands: how does the consumer-goods sector acquire its profits?*

The consumer-goods sector *did* make a profit in 1980—and in every other year since 1932. The reason is that the household sector has income in addition to the wages it receives from the consumer-goods sector.

Let us now recognize that the capital-goods sector exists. It paid its employees approximately $245 billion in 1980. If the people who received this income also spent every cent that they earned, the consumer-goods sector would have receipts of $245 billion in excess of its payroll costs—a profit on these costs, as the profit meter in Fig. 9 informs us.

Now that we are beginning to identify the sources of profits of the consumer-goods sector, it is handy to have a table where we can keep track of them:

| | |
|---|---|
| **wages and salaries paid by capital-goods sector** | **+ $245 billion** |
| | − |
| | + |
| | + |
| | + |
| | − |
| | + |
| | + |
| **consumer-goods-sector profits** | **$245 billion** |

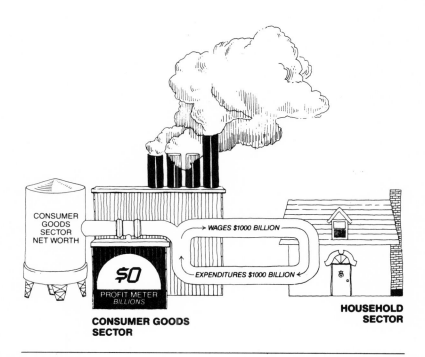

Figure 8. If the only source of consumer purchasing power were consumer-goods-sector wages, the sector could never make a profit, even if consumers spent every cent they earned!

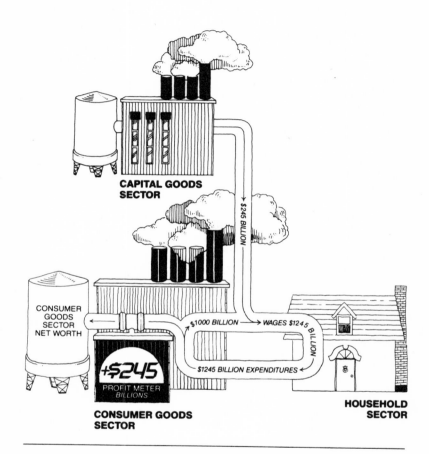

Figure 9. Capital-goods-sector wages, when spent by consumers, become consumer-goods-sector profits. In 1980, this source contributed an estimated $245 billion.

We have been assuming that consumers spend every penny they earn. In reality, of course, most of us save. In 1980, we consumers saved tens of billions of dollars. Whether these funds were invested, left in savings accounts at banks, put into bonds, or hidden under mattresses does not matter. As long as consumers did not spend this money, it could not become part of the receipts of the consumer-goods sector.

Figure 10 depicts savings as money that consumers withhold from the consumer-goods sector by storing it in the "consumer savings tank." When income flowing into the household sector is diverted into this tank, it does not flow to the consumer-goods sector as expenditures for goods and services. On the other hand, while most consumers add more to the tank each year, some "dissave"— that is, draw more funds out of the tank than they put in. (Of course, they must have saved this money previously.) In the United States since 1933, more money has been put into the tank annually than has been taken out. In other words, saving has been greater than dissaving.

But consumers are profligate as well as frugal. Many of them borrow to finance purchases ranging from trips to Hawaii to new vacuum cleaners. Even in the recession year 1980, consumer debt increased (consumers borrowed more than they paid back on old loans). The overall effect was an increase in the number of dollars that the household sector spent.

Figure 10 pictures consumer credit as a well. When consumers borrow, they draw money from the well. When they pay off old debts, they pour money back in. Usually, the net flow is out of the well.

The combined effect of saving, dissaving, borrowing, and liquidating old debt is that more money flows into the household sector than flows out. The Department of Commerce labels the total effect "personal saving." Figure 10 shows how four pipes converge into one (net) personal-saving pipe. (Of course, financial institutions pipe money from the savings tank to the credit well, but only the flows shown in Fig. 10 affect the household sector's expenditures for the products of the consumer-goods sector.)

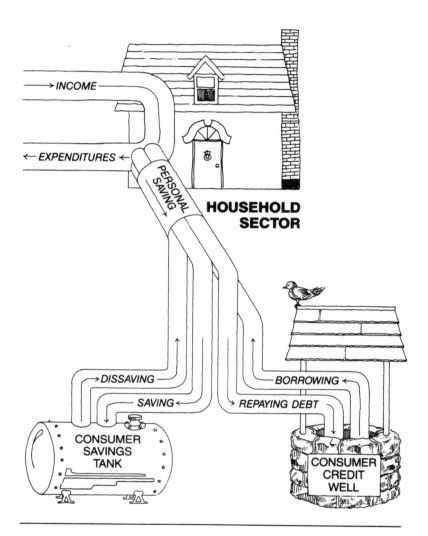

Figure 10. Saving, dissaving, borrowing, and repaying debt are all activities that affect how much of the household-sector income will flow out as expenditures. Personal saving, the official name given to the net effect of all of these transactions, generally reduces consumer expenditures.

In 1980, personal saving was $101 billion. Since the consumer-goods sector received $101 billion less in receipts as a result of this saving, profits were reduced by this amount, as shown in Fig. 11. Thus, personal saving is a *negative* source of profits:

| | |
|---|---|
| **wages and salaries paid by capital-goods sector** | **+ $245 billion** |
| **personal saving** | **− 101** |
| | **+** |
| | **+** |
| | **+** |
| | **−** |
| | **+** |
| | **+** |
| **consumer-goods-sector profits** | **$144 billion** |

Another source of profits is in the government sector. From one economic viewpoint, government is a purchasing agent for the people. It buys goods and services that they would have difficulty obtaining as individuals—highways, police protection, education, intercontinental ballistic missiles, sewage disposal, and countless other goods and services. So people let government take some of their money, mostly by taxation.

Government buys goods and services from the consumer-goods sector. (Recall that any finished goods not used by business are consumer goods—even submarines or courthouses.) The consumer-goods sector does not care whether money reaches it directly from the household sector or takes a detour through the government sector.

But not all government expenditures are for consumer goods. Government gives some funds right back to the household sector. For example, the federal government sends social security benefits to more than 30 million people. It also pays unemployment insurance, gives aid to poor persons with dependent children, and so forth. Money taxed from individuals and then transferred back to the household sector merely reshuffles income among consumers. The total dollar purchasing power of the household sector is unaffected.

Government is also an employer; it pays wages and salaries. This compensation is another way it returns income to the household

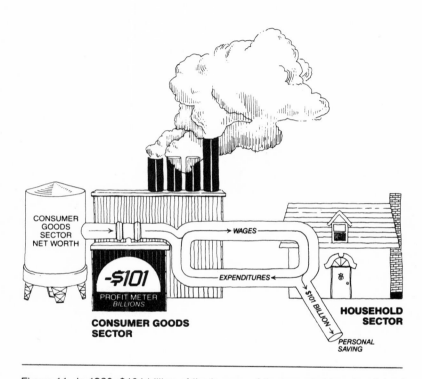

Figure 11. In 1980, $101 billion of the income of the household sector did not flow to the consumer-goods sector as consumer expenditures because it was detoured into the personal-savings pipe. Profits were reduced by $101 billion.

sector. Taxing the household sector and then returning tax money to it as wages does not affect the number of dollars the household sector has for spending.

What, then, is the effect on the profits of the consumer-goods sector if the government sector spends exactly what it collects from the household sector? No effect whatsoever. The government sector simply adds a loop to the flows of money through the economy (Fig. 12).

Of course, government taxes and expenditures are not always equal. When government takes more money away from consumers than it spends, it reduces the receipts of the consumer-goods sector. This net inflow is generally called "government surplus," which is another name for government saving. (Note that we are referring to the government sector, not just the federal government but the aggregation of all governments—federal, state, and local.)

The effect of government saving on the profits of the consumer-goods sector is the same as the effect of household saving. Whether consumers themselves save or government acting as their "purchasing agent" saves, the money will not reach the consumer-goods sector. Thus, a government surplus, like personal saving, would be a negative source of profits.

In 1980, the government had a deficit; its outlays exceeded its receipts. In other words, the government borrowed. Thus, it added to the flow of funds into the consumer-goods sector; it contributed to the sector's profits. A government deficit is always a positive source of consumer-goods-sector profits.

The federal government had a deficit of $61 billion in 1980, and the state and local governments a collective surplus of $29 billion. The entire government sector therefore had a $32-billion deficit. Figure 13 shows how this deficit increased the profits of the consumer-goods sector.

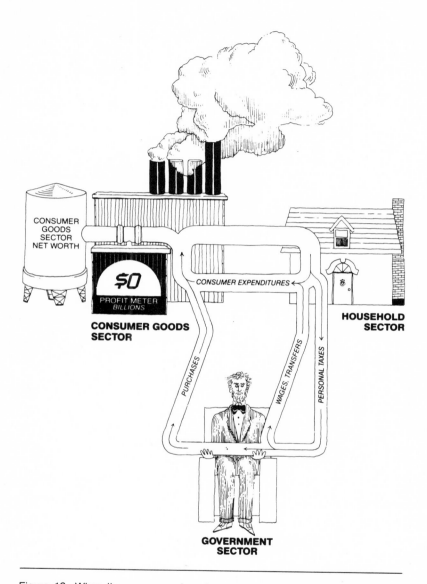

Figure 12. When the government sector spends exactly what it collects from the household sector, it simply adds a loop to the flow of money to the consumer-goods sector. It therefore does not affect profits.

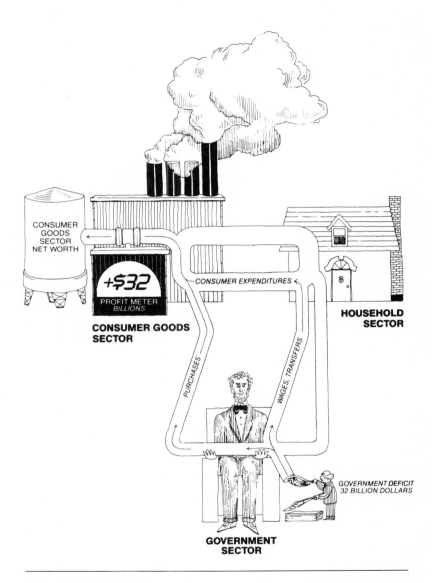

Figure 13. A government-sector deficit adds money to the consumer-goods-sector revenue, but not to expenses. Therefore it adds directly to profits. In 1980, this source contributed $32 billion to the consumer-goods sector's profits.

Now we can add another line to our table:

| | |
|---|---|
| wages and salaries paid by capital-goods sector | + $245 billion |
| personal saving (−) | − 101 |
| government surplus (−), or deficit (+) | + 32 |
| | + |
| | + |
| | − |
| | + |
| | + |
| consumer-goods-sector profits | $176 billion |

We have seen that whether consumers spend or save is critical to the consumer-goods sector. But so is *how* they spend. Sometimes consumers buy a Fiat, a Nikon camera, or a ticket on Air France. Domestic business is then deprived of their money. Some of the wages paid to the household sector by American businesses do not return to the consumer-goods sector as expenditures for domestic goods and services. Instead, these funds leave the country as purchases of foreign goods and services. Such transactions—imports, purchases by Americans traveling abroad, and so forth—reduce profits.

Profits are further decreased when the consumer-goods sector imports raw materials, parts, and other inventory goods. When American firms pay for these items, money flows directly from the consumer-goods sector to the foreign sector, perhaps never to be seen again. Profits are reduced by the amount of these imports. Fortunately for the consumer-goods sector, foreign nations—governments, businesses, individuals—buy many American products. Money flows from abroad into the consumer-goods sector.

There are scores of other kinds of transactions that bring additional money into the country, or that take money out. For example, some of our consumers have income from abroad—wages, salaries, interest, dividends, and so forth. On the other hand, a small fraction of the income created in the United States is paid to foreigners. For example, Japanese citizens work in the U.S. Embassy in Tokyo.

A pipeline diagram of all these international transactions that affect consumer-goods-sector profits would look like a bowl of spaghetti. Yet they can all be summarized by a single term, "consumer net foreign investment." When this term is positive, more money is coming into the consumer-goods sector from abroad than is flowing out, adding to the sector's profits. When the net flow is out of the country, these profits are reduced.

Figure 14 illustrates two of the most important kinds of foreign transactions: imports of consumer goods and services by the household sector, and purchases of similar products from domestic businesses by foreign nations. If these two flows were equal, there would be no overall impact on the profits of the consumer-goods sector. A much more complicated, "bowl of spaghetti" version of Fig. 14 would include all the other types of transactions in consumer net foreign investment. It also would show that a perfect balance results in a zero addition to the profits of the American consumer-goods sector.

Estimating that in 1980 consumer net foreign investment was \$4 billion, we add this profit source to our table:

| | |
|---|---|
| wages and salaries paid by capital-goods sector | + \$245 billion |
| personal saving (−) | − 101 |
| government surplus (−), or deficit (+) | + 32 |
| consumer net foreign investment | + 4 |
| | + |
| | − |
| | + |
| | + |
| consumer-goods-sector profits | \$180 billion |

We said earlier that all of the wages paid by the consumer-goods sector are expenses. Now we must amend that statement. Some of those wage expenses are canceled out by a gain of the consumer-goods sector, the accumulation of valuable inventory goods. Let's take a closer look.

Inventory goods, as defined earlier, include raw materials, parts, supplies, and finished goods awaiting sale that are held by businesses. Usually the consumer-goods sector increases its holdings of inventory goods during the year. Workers are paid to produce these goods even though the consumer-goods sector does not sell them.

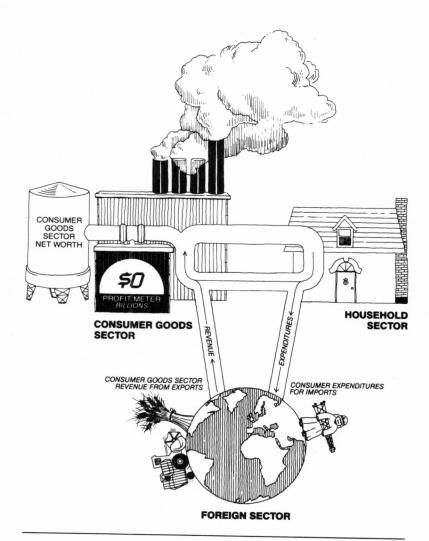

Figure 14. Pictured are two of the most important international transactions that affect the profits of the consumer-goods sector. They are imports of consumer goods and services by the household sector, and exports of similar products. If these two flows were equal, the overall impact on the profits of the consumer-goods sector would be nil.

The view of this situation generally taken by accountants is that the value of the workers' efforts is stored in these inventory goods. As long as a firm is accumulating valuable inventory goods at the same time that it is paying out wages, it is not losing any of its wealth; it is merely transferring its holdings from cash into another form of property. Later, when the inventory goods are sold, the firm and its accountants recognize that an expense has been incurred.

So far we have counted all of the wages paid by the consumer-goods sector as expenses. Now we make an adjustment. Like the accountants referred to above, we are not going to consider the wages paid for the production of inventory goods as an expense of the consumer-goods sector. This reduction in expenses is also an increase in profits.

Perhaps an example will help give an intuitive sense of why increased inventories add to profits. Suppose you owned a company that manufactures pottery. At the beginning of the year you had $10,000 in cash and $25,000 worth of pottery in stock. After a year of making ceramics, selling them, and paying employees, rent, and other operating expenses, you ended up with $10,000 in cash and *$50,000* worth of pottery. Your accountant would assure you that you had a profit of $25,000 and the Internal Revenue Service would insist that you did, even though all of your gains were invested in inventory.

In 1980, consumer-goods-sector inventories increased in value by about $32 billion, and we add this source of profits to our table:

| | |
|---|---|
| wages and salaries paid by capital-goods sector | + $245 billion |
| personal saving (−) | − 101 |
| government surplus (−), or deficit (+) | + 32 |
| consumer net foreign investment | + 4 |
| changes in inventory of consumer-goods sector | + 32 |
| | − |
| | + |
| | + |
| consumer-goods-sector profits | $212 billion |

Factory and office buildings, vehicles, machines, furniture, and other capital goods of the consumer-goods sector continually wear out and become less valuable. This loss of value is accounted for by depreciation, a business expense. Even though no money changes hands, depreciation is an expense that reduces profits (see Fig. 15). It is covered by the term "capital consumption allowances" in the Department of Commerce's accounts.

In 1980, the capital consumption allowances of the consumer-goods sector were an estimated $201 billion. We accordingly add capital consumption allowances to our table as a negative source of profits:

| | |
|---|---:|
| wages and salaries paid by capital-goods sector | + $245 billion |
| personal saving (−) | − 101 |
| government surplus (−), or deficit (+) | + 32 |
| consumer net foreign investment | + 4 |
| changes in inventory of consumer-goods sector | + 32 |
| capital consumption allowances of consumer-goods sector (−) | − 201 |
| | + |
| | + |
| consumer-goods-sector profits | + 11 billion |

As business secures profits, it distributes some of them as dividends to its shareholders who are members of the household sector. Surprising as it may sound, these dividends are a source of new consumer-goods-sector profits! They result in revenue that does not have an offsetting expense. The revenue arises when consumers spend dividend income on goods and services, adding to the flow of money from the household sector to the consumer-goods sector. But no firm—in either the capital- or consumer-goods sector—incurs an expense when it pays dividends.

This concept—that dividends contribute to profits—may seem incongruous at first because people primarily think of dividends as a result of profits. For example, investors frequently try to anticipate what will happen to a company's dividends as a result of a change in its profits. But rarely does an investor, or anyone else, consider what happens to the money that he receives as dividends and then spends for personal consumption. Because of the dynamic nature of the economy, dividends paid by either the capital- or consumer-goods sector flow to the household sector and then circulate back

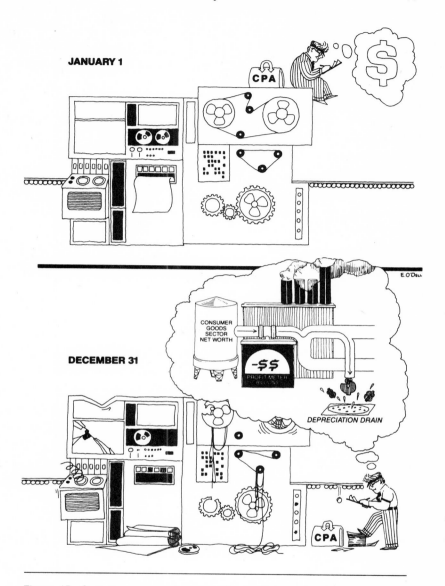

Figure 15. Over the course of a year, the capital goods of the consumer-goods sector lose value as a result of wear, tear, and age. The sector's net worth decreases. Accountants take note of this decline by deducting capital consumption allowances from net worth, almost as if money were flowing out of the expense pipe and going down the drain.

to the consumer-goods sector to become *new* profits.

Figure 16 illustrates this process. Starting in the capital-goods and consumer-goods sectors, dividend payments flow out of the net worth storage tanks and over to shareholders in the household sector. Notice that dividends, unlike wages and other expenses, do not pass out of the consumer- (or capital-) goods sector by flowing backward through the profit pipeline, registering a negative number on the profit meter, and then exiting via the expense pipe. Instead, these payments go directly to the household sector. Next, the recipients spend their dividend income, which becomes revenue for the consumer-goods sector—and, since there is no offsetting expense, profits. (Although consumers do not spend all of their dividend income, we already accounted for the part they save—as well as the part of wages they save—when we acknowledged personal saving as a negative source of profits.)

This process does not have a start or a finish; it is a continuing, circular flow of money. As you look at Fig. 16, imagine money flowing like water around and around through the pipes, all the time registering more and more dollars on the profit meter. In 1980, business paid $56 billion in dividends and these funds cycled around to become new consumer-goods-sector profits.

When we discussed the government sector, we ignored profits taxes. Uncle Sam is a kind of uninvited partner who moved in on the stockholders of every corporation—like a not-always-agreeable guest who came to visit and forgot to go home. Even worse, he brought with him many of the state governments. These not-so-welcome partners, in effect, declare dividends for themselves to be paid from the profits of corporations. Their "dividends" are larger than those that go to the stockholders who have risked their capital. The "dividends" appropriated by government are profits taxes.

Profits taxes, like conventional dividends, are not considered an expense. Of course, this doesn't mean that stockholders like them any more than expenses. Indeed, investment decisions usually take into consideration what profits will be *after tax.*

Profits taxes and dividends flow through similar pipelines. Dividends are paid to the household sector and then flow to the con-

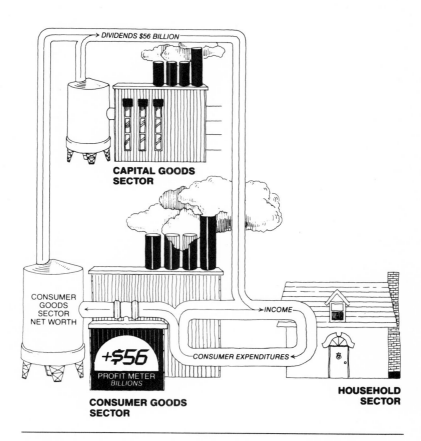

Figure 16. Dividends are not business expenses, but they become revenue of the consumer-goods sector when they flow from the household sector as consumer expenditures. Thus, they add to consumer-goods-sector profits. In 1980, this contribution to profits was $56 billion.

sumer-goods sector. Profits taxes are paid to the government sector and then they, too, flow to the consumer-goods sector.

In 1980, profits taxes were $82 billion. Figure 17 shows how these funds contributed to profits.

Behold the completed table of the profits of the consumer-goods sector:

| | |
|---|---|
| wages and salaries paid by capital-goods sector | + $245 billion |
| personal saving (−) | −   101 |
| government surplus (−), or deficit (+) | +    32 |
| consumer net foreign investment | +     4 |
| changes in inventory of consumer-goods sector | +    32 |
| capital consumption allowances of consumer-goods sector (−) | −   201 |
| dividends | +    56 |
| corporate profits taxes | +    82 |
| | |
| consumer-goods-sector profits | $149 billion |

Now that the profits of the consumer-goods sector have been traced, it is a small task to find those of the capital-goods sector.

### THE PROFITS OF THE CAPITAL-GOODS SECTOR

The capital-goods sector sells goods to itself and to the consumer-goods sector. We refer to its revenue by the name that the Department of Commerce uses, "fixed investment." The money for these purchases comes from corporate treasuries or is borrowed. But to the purchaser the outlay of cash for a capital good is not an expense.

The major expense of the capital-goods sector is its wage (including salary) costs. We now start a new table, still using 1980 figures:

| | |
|---|---|
| fixed investment | + $401 billion |
| capital-goods-sector wages and salaries (−) | −   245 |
| | + |
| | + |
| | − |
| | |
| capital-goods-sector profits | $156 billion |

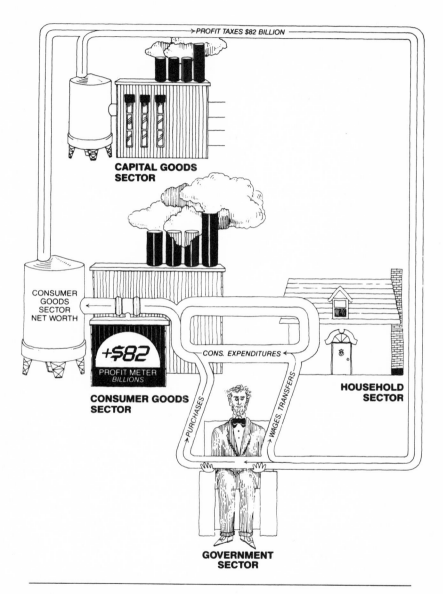

Figure 17. Profits taxes are not business expenses, but they become revenue of the consumer-goods sector when the government sector spends them. Thus, they add to consumer-goods-sector profits. In 1980, this contribution amounted to $82 billion.

"Fixed investment" largely represents American business's purchases of capital goods from domestic industry. But many capital goods are purchased from the foreign sector. Some U.S. companies buy, for example, Mercedes-Benz trucks or Hitachi industrial robots. Thus imports reduce the revenues of the capital-goods sector. In addition, this sector imports raw materials, components, and other items, which add to its expenses.

But this sector, like the consumer-goods sector, increases its revenues by selling some of its products to the foreign sector. Boeing 747s, Sperry Corporation computers, and Cincinnati milling machines are used all over the world. The net effect of all these international transactions on the capital-goods sector is summarized under the term: "capital goods net foreign investment." In 1980, it amounted to $2 billion.

The capital-goods sector, like the consumer-goods sector, carries inventory goods—fuel, raw materials, parts, finished goods waiting to be sold, and so forth. It, too, profits when the value of its inventories increases. In 1980, this gain was about $8 billion.

The capital-goods sector also has capital consumption allowances. In 1980, these were about $70 billion.

We can now complete our table:

| | |
|---|---|
| fixed investment | + $401 billion |
| capital-goods sector wages and salaries (−) | − 245 |
| capital-goods net foreign investment | + 2 |
| change in inventory, capital-goods sector | + 8 |
| capital consumption allowances (−) | − 70 |
| capital-goods-sector profits | $ 96 billion |

## THE PROFITS OF THE BUSINESS SECTOR

Earlier, we divided the business sector into two parts. Without this division, we would not have been able to see many of the flows of money that are important parts of the process by which profits are generated.

As a consequence of splitting the business sector, we now have not one but two lists of profit sources. To complete our task and produce a single list of the sources of profits for the entire business sector, we have only to combine those of the two subsectors. The table below shows the profit sources of the consumer-goods sector in the first column, the profit sources of the capital-goods sector in the second, and their sum—the profit sources of the entire business sector—in the third:

| (billions of dollars) | consumer-goods sector | + capital-goods sector = | business sector |
|---|---|---|---|
| fixed investment | | +$401 | +$401 |
| capital-goods-sector wages & salaries | +$245 | − 245 | |
| *personal saving* | − 101 | | − 101 |
| *government surplus (−),* deficit (+) | + 32 | | + 32 |
| net foreign investment | + 4 | + 2 | + 6 |
| change in inventory | + 32 | + 8 | + 40 |
| *capital consumption allowances* | − 201 | − 70 | − 270 |
| dividends | + 56 | | + 56 |
| corporate profit taxes | + 82 | | + 82 |
| **total profits** | **+$149** | **+$ 96 =** | **$245** |

(Terms in italics are negative sources of total business-sector profits.)

The third column, the business-sector profit sources, is exactly the list we derived in chapter 4 from the saving-investment equation:

corporate profits before tax    =    + fixed investment
+ change in business inventories
+ net foreign investment
− personal saving
− capital consumption allowances
− government surplus or + deficit
+ dividends
+ corporate profits tax

Now that we have a general understanding of how money flows around the economy, enabling business to secure profits, the going will be less technical. The time has come to put our discoveries to good use.

# 6

# Three Myths About Profits

Armed with knowledge of the sources of profits, we are ready to begin a hunting expedition that will occupy us for much of the remainder of this book. Our prey: myths about profits and the economy.

In this chapter, we will go after three myths that are more than curiosities. Each is a fundamental misunderstanding about profits that has caused poor economic policymaking, destructive behavior by investors and workers, and even war. We must bury these erroneous concepts if we are to meet the economic challenges that face the nation and the world.

## Myth: The Total Amount of Profits in the Economy Depends on Business Greed

Millions of Americans—and countless other people around the world—mistakenly believe that profits are the result of rapaciousness. In their view, business gets profits that it does not deserve. It is "guilty" of somehow taking money that rightfully belongs to workers or consumers. Many people believe that the profits of business thus depend on the greed of its investors and managers, and on how much society allows them to get away with.

Business allegedly steals profits from society in many ways. It underpays workers and overcharges customers. It misrepresents the dangers of the products it sells and misleads with its advertising. Its members conspire to eliminate competition. In these and other devious ways, business manages to obtain much higher profits than it should.

In reality, the business sector's total amount of profits has little to do with how far corporations overstep the bounds of justice and ethics. Yes, sometimes enterprises do engage in undesirable practices. Some of them do get profits that they do not deserve. Yet these actions hardly affect the *total* amount of profits in the economy; they primarily affect the distribution of these profits—that is, which firms get how much. If some companies secure additional profits by cheating customers or anyone else, other businesses must receive less.

We have seen that there is a finite amount of profits generated in the economy every year, an amount equal to the flows from the profit sources. If business could increase its aggregate profits by cheating, such malfeasance would have to alter these flows; the profit sources would have to be affected.

Cheating can increase total profits only slightly, at most. More likely, if firms were allowed to conduct their affairs without fear of the antitrust laws or statutes that protect their customers, employees, and the environment, total profits in the nation would decline!

Imagine the United States was a land where neither laws nor conscience restrained business people in their quests for profits. A commercial would promise toddlers that smoking cigarettes would give them big muscles and make them tall. The presidents of large corporations would meet regularly to fix prices and divide markets. All warranties would be avoided by the fine print. *Caveat emptor,* not *E Pluribus Unum,* would adorn the nation's coins. Life in this imaginary America would leave a great deal to be desired. The national standard of living would be lower, death and injury more frequent, and frustration widespread. But what about profits? Let's look at the list of sources:

> fixed investment
> changes in business inventories
> net foreign investment
> − personal saving
> − capital consumption allowances
> − government surplus (or + deficit)
> dividends
> corporate profits tax

Fixed investment, ordinarily the largest of the profit sources, would fall! Consider the case of a widget manufacturer with two-year-old production facilities that should last another ten years. Suppose it is contemplating an investment in a brand-new production process that would lower costs 10% per unit and turn out a superior widget. In a competitive environment, the manufacturer would install the new machinery. The company could not afford to let its competitors obtain an edge by modernizing first. However, in our imaginary economy run by cutthroats and thieves, all the widget manufacturers would collude. They would fix prices, divide the market, prevent new firms from entering the industry, and otherwise thwart the competition. The company with the two-year-old equipment would see no reason to rush into a major investment, go to all the trouble of changing over its production process, and suffer other trauma and inconvenience—even if it would be able to cut costs. As long as it was guaranteed its share of the market and high price, it would feel little pressure to update or improve its operations. Similarly, investment would be low in industries throughout the economy. The nation's aggregate profits would be reduced accordingly.

How about inventories? An absence of government regulation or business scruples would not affect this source of profits. Businesses expand their inventories as much as they like. Prudence, not regulation or conscience, restricts inventories.

Nor would business hanky-panky be likely to increase net foreign investment. If firms were lackadaisical about improving their efficiency and their products, fewer American goods would find export markets. Meanwhile, foreign goods would become more attractive to American buyers. Imports would probably rise. The most likely result would therefore be a decrease in net foreign investment. An increase in this profit source would be highly improbable.

Another possible way for business to increase its profits would be to reduce personal saving. But could price-fixing and skulduggery induce consumers to save less? Maybe a little. But saving might increase. Even though the saving rate is not always the same, we cannot predict how, or whether, business shenanigans would affect it. Nevertheless, the effect of a dramatic increase in what are generally regarded as fraudulent or unlawful business practices would be unlikely to change consumers' traditional attitudes toward saving.

Continuing down the list of profit sources, we come to capital consumption allowances. This item reflects real losses in the value of plant and equipment. No matter how dishonest or greedy a business executive may be, he cannot influence the deleterious effects of friction, stress, and corrosion on structures and machines. Of course, if firms invested less in new plant and equipment because of reduced competition, their depreciation costs would gradually decrease over a period of years.

If business were to get what it typically advocates, lower profits taxes and a reduced government deficit, its profits would fall both before and after taxes. Both corporate profits tax and government deficit are sources of profits.

Only one other source of profits remains: dividends. But government places no constraints on the amount of dividends that corporations can pay. Thus, unrestrained cheating and greed would not increase dividends.

To summarize, we found only two conceivable ways that business machinations could increase profits: by increasing net foreign investment and by reducing personal saving. Yet both of these would probably change in the other direction, and reduce profits. Furthermore, expected changes in fixed investment, profits tax, and the government deficit would decrease profits. All in all, aggregate profits could not rise much; they would probably fall significantly.

So much for the greed-makes-profits myth. Interestingly enough, it has a cousin that also asserts that business is responsible for its own profitability. This cousin, the efficiency-makes-profits myth, is popular among proponents of capitalism, and is just as fallacious as its anticapitalist relative. The reasoning that exposes it is similar to the argument presented above: firms cannot alter the federal government's deficit, corporate tax rates, or the personal saving rate by being efficient any more than they can by being unscrupulous. The remaining profit sources can at best only explain how a tiny part of aggregate profits result from business efficiency.

Efficiency may affect attitudes and expectations that bear on the profit sources, but efficiency itself is not linked to the nation's flow of profits. During every recession, when profits drop more than 20%, no comparable decline occurs in business efficiency!

What does increase profits is the investment in capital goods that often raises efficiency. For example, when a manager discovers how he can automate his production line and speed up operations, he is likely to order new machines. But *any* changes that call for additional investment—even if they *lower* efficiency—will increase total profits. When the manager buys new pollution-control devices that reduce the efficiency of his plant, the investment increases total business-sector profits. Of course, the company that lost efficiency might lose profits, but others would gain.

Many business people blame government regulations for causing inefficiency and therefore reducing profits. Without such interference, they argue, business-sector profits would be higher. Yet the connection between government regulations and total business profits is tenuous. Some regulations, such as those prohibiting the construction of plants without extensive environmental-impact studies, inhibit investment and therefore reduce profits. Others, such as pollution-control laws, require plants to invest in special equipment that they would not otherwise buy. These laws increase profits. For the most part, regulations, whatever their effect on efficiency, do not have a significant impact on the total amount of profits secured by the business sector.

Why have both the greed-makes-profits and the efficiency-makes-profits myths gained widespread acceptance? Because people have observed that a *single* firm often profits by circumventing the law or by increasing its efficiency. If all companies behaved this way, they reason, total profits would rise.

*However, no firm can make its own profits. It can only win some of those generated by the economy.* Since the flow of profits into the economy at any time is finite, when one firm increases its share, others must suffer. Earlier we said that profits are, in a way, like prizes offered to children in school. No student can increase the total number of prizes offered; he can only strive to win as many of those that are available as he can. If he succeeds in winning a prize by cheating in a contest, he is depriving another pupil of his reward. The number of prizes is unchanged.

So if one firm cheats its workers, customers, or society in general—and gets away with its transgression—it siphons additional profits away from other companies. Or, if it succeeds in raising its efficiency more than its rivals, it can win more profits. *However, the total amount of profits available to all firms in the business sector is beyond the control of individual enterprises.*

## Myth: Socialist and Communist Countries Can and Have Successfully Eliminated Profits

Profits, according to Karl Marx, incarnate the fundamental injustice of capitalism. They arise, he said, because the prices capitalists charge for goods exceed the wages paid to the workers who produce the goods. The true value of any product, Marx maintained, is equal to the cost of the labor that produces it. Profits represent "surplus value" that is skimmed off by capitalists but rightfully belongs to workers.

Instead of this "unjust" economic system, Marx prescribed an economy in which production would be centrally planned and controlled. Prices of goods and services would be exactly equal to the labor costs incurred in production. Eventually, the economy would mature into an ideal society with no need for money. In this paradise, people would consume what they needed without having to worry about prices.

Many socialists agree with Marx's explanation of profits even though they may disagree with him on other points. Like Marx, they think that an economy should be run without profits.

Today, a number of nations around the world have economies that are primarily socialist. (We take our definition of "socialism" from the *Webster's Third New International Dictionary:* "a system or condition of society in which the means of production are owned and controlled by the state.") Yet there is no viable national economy on earth that does not have profits! At most, a government can disguise profits; eliminating them is not feasible.

Profits inevitably arise in any economy that is not on the brink of collapse. Whether it is capitalist, socialist, democratic, totalitarian, industrialized, developing, homogeneous, heterogeneous, vegetarian, or cannibalistic makes no difference. Profits will be there.

The Soviet Union seems an appropriate choice for a demonstration that even Communist countries have profits. The existence of profits in the land of long winters and abundant vodka is beyond doubt; the USSR actually publishes profit data along with other statistics available in the West. Using the Soviet Union as an example, and knowledge about the sources of profits, we can explain how profits arise in an economy whether anyone wants them or not—even in the world's greatest pulpit for anticapitalist rhetoric and the site of history's first Marxist revolution.

The Bolsheviks who led the October revolution in 1917 may have had every intention of creating the utopian society that Marx had described. However, their initial attempt to reform the economy resulted in disaster. It occurred during the civil war that followed the revolution, and appropriately became known as "War Communism." Under this program, which was an uneven application of Marx's principles, the national product plummeted and misery became widespread.

Lenin initiated the New Economic Policy (NEP) in 1921 to save the prostrate economy. NEP was a partial retreat toward capitalism, for it tolerated substantial amounts of free market trade and private profits. Under this program, the Soviet Union was able to struggle back to its knees.

Not until 1928 did the government completely take the operation of the economy into its own hands. In that year, Stalin introduced the first of the famous "five-year plans" and the state began to dictate what would be produced where, when, and by whom. Even though the Soviet economy had not yet fulfilled the hopes of the revolutionaries, the state now had the power, authority, and will to implement true socialism.

As Stalin's rule began, orthodox Communists in the Kremlin probably expected that they had seen the last of that scourge of capitalism, profits. But they were in for a lesson in economics. Not only did profits persist in the Soviet Union, they soared to heights never dreamed of even in the days of the czars. Eventually, the Communist party leaders must have resigned themselves to the existence of profits. Apparently they decided that profits were all right as long as the state collected them. Getting rid of them posed too many problems.

Why did profits arise in the Soviet Union? Were they the result of Communists' failure to adhere to the doctrines of Karl Marx? Many Marxists may be inclined to think so. Yet no matter how carefully the revolutionaries had followed the advice of the economist-philosopher, and no matter how successful the Soviet economy might have become, profits would have been present. The forces that generate profits know no ideology.

To one who knows where profits come from, it is not necessary to see Russian economic statistics to surmise that the Soviet Union is rolling in profits. The USSR's great emphasis on expanding its industrial base and enlarging its economy makes large profits inevitable. The sources of profits explain why.

All of these sources represent activities that take place in the Soviet Union as well as in the United States—all, that is, except one. In Russia, there are no distributions of profits to private investors— no dividends. However, this difference does not mean that we cannot use what we have learned about the generation of profits to analyze the Soviet economy. Nor does the ownership of business by the government complicate our task. The Soviet Union has the same sectors we discussed in the previous chapter.

The most crucial source of profits in the USSR is fixed investment. Soviet investment, especially since Stalin announced the first five-year plan in 1928, has been enormous compared to the production of consumer goods and services. Stalin paid little heed to those who urged increasing the output of consumer products in order to relieve the miserable conditions under which most citizens lived. Instead, he sought to catch up with the West by placing the highest priority on developing an industrial base. Great proportions of Soviet gross national product represented investment in steel mills, railroads, mines, heavy machinery, and other capital goods.

Think back to our "pipeline economy" in chapter 5. Recall how the wages paid by the capital-goods sector added to consumers' purchasing power, and thus to consumer-goods-sector profits (Fig. 9, page 62). A similar diagram of the Soviet economy would show a much larger capital-goods sector with a far greater proportional impact on consumer purchasing power.

A problem developed early in Soviet history because the government wanted the prices of consumer goods to approximate their costs. The people's purchasing power in rubles greatly exceeded the total price of the available scanty supplies of consumer items. Long lines of consumers with money that they could find no way to spend appeared the moment anything was offered for sale.

If this situation occurred in a capitalist system, markets would rapidly boost prices until a balance existed between the quantity of goods and services for sale and the amount of money consumers wanted to spend. But in the USSR, government-mandated prices did not change in response to consumer demand. People were forced to save by the absence of opportunities to spend their money.

When people are forced to save huge portions of their incomes and are given little reason to hope that they will ever be able to spend their savings, bad things start to happen. Money loses value. Black markets spring up. People become disillusioned. The system starts to crumble.

If the Soviet officials had persisted with their pricing schedules and thereby forced people to save, they could have prevented profits from occurring—that is, until their economy collapsed. Personal saving, a negative profit source, would have been unreasonably large. It could have offset the enormous flows of profits generated by fixed investment. But this policy would have destroyed the economy as money became completely meaningless and consumer frustration dangerously aggravated.

Instead, the Soviet leaders did what they had to do: they raised prices in order to drain off excess consumer purchasing power. They allowed the state-owned businesses to make large profits.

We have talked only about two of the sources of Soviet profits—fixed investment and personal saving (a negative source). What about the others? Do one or more of them hold a key that would have enabled the Soviet leaders to eliminate profits?

The items in question are:

> change in business inventories
> net foreign investment
> — capital consumption allowances
> — government surplus (or + deficit)
> profits tax

The change in business inventories can be rejected immediately. To prevent profits, the state's businesses would have had to permit their inventories to *decline* by an incredible amount every year. Even if officials had been willing to pursue such a ridiculous strategy, their inventories would have been rapidly reduced to nothing. Then what?

Net foreign investment could not have been used to reduce profits, either. To offset the profits created by the investment in capital goods, this source of profits would have had to be negative. That would have meant vast amounts of money flowing out of the country every year. But virtually no one beyond the USSR's borders wanted rubles, so little Russian money could flow to foreign countries.

Capital consumption allowances (largely depreciation) certainly could not have offset profits. Remember, this negative profit source represents the loss in value of the nation's capital goods as they become old and run-down. In a growing economy—especially one with such enormous energies devoted to increasing its industrial base—these losses could never be anywhere near as large as new investment in capital goods. But that investment is the very source of profits the Soviets would have had to offset.

What about profits taxes? For the government to tax profits, there would have to *be* profits! Goods would have to be sold to consumers for more than their labor costs. If the government levied a 100% profits tax, and retained this money (ran a surplus), it *could* take profits out of the hands of its enterprises. But in this case, it would not be preventing profits—just gathering them up and hiding them!

Theoretically, the government could tax 100% of consumers' excess purchasing power, and apparently eliminate profits. It would have to run an enormous surplus in order to keep this money from contributing to profits; it would have to accumulate vast amounts of money that it would never spend.

But if the government had constantly drawn huge sums of money out of the economy and into its treasury, would it really have eliminated profits? Would it then have itself become the recipient of "surplus value"? By transferring gains from state enterprises into other official accounts, government would have succeeded only in disguising profits, not eliminating them. A continuing, unnecessary accumulation of funds by government can be viewed as nothing more than a bookkeeping trick. Without such sleight of hand no economy, even one run by the state, can offer all consumer goods and services to workers at prices equal to labor costs. Marx's prescription is naïve.

The Soviet Union lives with its profits. No government can survive if it is ñot realistic, and the USSR has survived for more than half a century. If you can't beat 'em, join 'em, so profits are an accepted part of the Soviet economy. A large part of these profits is taxed away by the "turnover tax," a levy on consumer goods. The government also declares itself "dividends," which are not dividends as we know them under capitalism, but a profits tax. And still, Soviet enterprises are left with substantial undistributed profits.

As we bury the myth that profits are purely a capitalist phenomenon, it is interesting to reflect back on two myths already interred: "Greed makes profits" and "Efficiency makes profits." The Soviet Union is a wonderful contradiction to both. It has neither greedy investors nor, as we mentioned earlier, efficiency; and yet its profits are abundant.

## Myth: An Increase in Total Wages Will Decrease Total Profits in the Economy

Now the time has come to vanquish one of the most popular, important economic myths of all, one that has been creating a great deal of mischief around the world. It is the myth that employee compensation rates affect the distribution of income between workers as a class and the owners of business as a class. It underlies the belief in the class struggle between workers and capitalists. It is responsible for distracting Americans, Britons, and other people from seeing some of the fundamental conflicts of interests that do exist. One of these conflicts is between workers who value leisure and consumers who crave goods and services. Another is the real struggle among groups of consumers over slices of economic pie. Instead of coming to grips with these important trade-offs, society tears itself apart in a phantom struggle between workers and capitalists.

Moreover, the myth obscures a crucial common interest of every member of society: maximizing productivity. Strikes, lockouts, apathy, poor management support for lower-level employees, and other sources of inefficiency can seriously hamper society's ability to produce goods and services. The class-struggle myth distorts the appearance of these destructive behaviors and makes them look like appropriate tactics for people trying to raise their standards of living.

Rising wages do not hurt the capitalist class; increases in pay rates actually *increase* profits. To aid in the exposition of this phenomenon, we introduce two nations. The first will be known as A-land, the second as B-land. The true identities of these countries will be revealed later.

A-land and B-land were once remarkably similar. They had no significant differences in area, population, climate, political system, culture, education, natural resources, and industrial development. Neither had the slightest edge over the other in technology, production facilities, work-force quality, international connections, or anything else that would have affected its economy. At the time we began to look at them, both had been enjoying moderate prosperity and reasonably stable prices.

But as of January 2, 19xx, they were never again the same. An amazing thing happened in B-land. No one is quite sure what caused it, but according to rumor a good fairy had enchanted the country. Whatever the reason, every employer in B-land raised the compensation rates of his employees by exactly 10%. Even the stingiest, most hardhearted scrooge felt himself strangely compelled to grant his employees raises. Most amazing were the 10% raises for government employees—congressmen, judges, and other officials— whose salaries were fixed by law. When the lawyers consulted the statute books, they found that the mandated salaries were 10% higher than anyone had remembered.

No worker was overlooked—blue-collar or white-collar, male or female, publicly or privately employed. Electricians, movie stars, teachers, musicians, construction workers, corporate executives, policemen, baby-sitters—all had something to celebrate early in the New Year.

Meanwhile, in A-land, compensation rates were stable. Wages, salaries, commissions, and fringe benefits remained the same as during the previous 12 months. The only people who received raises were those who advanced to higher-paying jobs.

However, there were no differences in the way people behaved in the two countries during the rest of the year. In both countries, managers continued to purchase new capital goods, enlarge their inventories, and compete for customers. Neither country employed more workers or produced more goods and services than the other.

The conduct of public affairs in the two nations continued to be identical. Both government sectors employed the same number of people to perform the same tasks. The goods and services purchased by government in A-land were indistinguishable from those in B-land. Each nation devoted the same proportion of its budget to social benefits, and the tax rates on profits, personal income, sales, and so forth were identical in the two countries.

Consumers continued to save at the same rates in both countries. In B-land, the majority of the people, who had 10% more income, spent 10% more and saved 10% more.

Nevertheless, some unusual phenomena occurred in B-land during the year. The first was inflation. Prices, which had been relatively stable for years, suddenly began to rise. They shot up dramatically early in the year, then began to level off. By the fourth quarter, when prices were fairly stable, they had increased by an average of 9%. As a result of the price increases, workers found that they could not enjoy much of an improvement in their standard of living. Even worse, retired people living on savings found that their purchasing power was seriously diminished.

But an even stranger development was what happened to profits. Despite fears that the pay increase would devastate business profits, business prospered. According to the accountants, profits rose 13% more in B-land than in A-land by the fourth quarter of 19xx.

To see what caused this astonishing increase, we start by investigating the impact of the pay increases on prices. An immediate consequence of the raise was an increase in consumer spending. Wages, salaries, and other employee compensation constitute the greatest part of personal income. (Personal income is the total income of all persons in the country—their wages, dividends, interest, social security, pension and welfare payments, and so forth.) Those who received these pay increases spent 10% more than their A-land counterparts. Since B-land did not produce any more consumer goods and services than A-land, more money was paid to the consumer-goods sector for the same goods. Inflation!

Once this inflation of consumer prices began, other factors added to it. For example, government paid higher social insurance and welfare payments. The national policy was to provide certain standards of living for the recipients of social-benefit payments. As prices rose, the government increased these transfer payments, adding even more to personal income. The prices of consumer goods and services continued to advance.

A small part of personal income did not rise with wages and salaries. For example, interest income did not rise as fast. The interest payments on outstanding bonds did not increase at all. However, interest rates on newly issued obligations were soon rising in response to inflation.

By the fourth quarter of 19xx, personal income had risen about 9% more in B-land than in A-land. Since the saving rates (saving as a percentage of income) were the same in both countries, consumer spending was 9% higher in B-land. Of course, the government sector, as well as the household sector, buys from the consumer-goods sector. Since the government in B-land bought the same goods and services as the one in A-land, its purchases, too, were higher as a result of inflation. By the fourth quarter, the total revenues of the consumer-goods sector had increased 9%. The inflation of consumer goods and services was, therefore, 9%.

Price increases were not limited to the consumer-goods sector. Inflation befell the capital-goods sector as well.

When the good fairy raised employee compensation 10%, she created a problem for the capital-goods sector. Its labor costs—the greatest part of its total expenses—suddenly jumped 10%. At current prices of capital goods, this situation spelled disaster to many firms. What would happen if they raised prices? Would they lose a substantial amount of sales?

No. Executives in the consumer-goods sector, which buys most of the product of the capital-goods sector, looked at their companies' financial performances. They noted that revenues were up 9%, and that the profit on each dollar of sales was, if anything, increasing. Business appeared to be so good that they were eager to buy capital goods even at higher prices.

In fact, capital goods in B-land were generally worth 9% more to consumer-goods-sector firms than were identical products in A-land. Consider, for example, a stamping machine. Prior to the pay increases, its annual production could be sold for $100,000. But with 9% inflation, the machine's yearly output was worth $109,000. Therefore, the machine was worth 9% more to its owners than formerly. The consumer-goods sector was willing to pay the higher prices that the capital-goods sector needed to charge.

The capital-goods-sector firms soon found that not only their labor costs but their own outlays for new plant and equipment were increasing. As a result, their depreciation expenses began to rise, and so the capital-goods sector raised its prices still further.

By the fourth quarter of 19xx, B-land capital-goods prices were about 9% higher than corresponding prices in A-land. The markets for capital goods, which had been disturbed by the pay increase and its consequences, had readjusted. (In academic parlance, what ultimately happened in the B-land capital-goods markets was an upward shift of 9% in the demand curve and an upward shift of about the same percentage in the supply curve. As a result, prices rose about 9% and volume did not change significantly.)

We begin to see that the pay increase did not decrease profits, because there really was not much of a pay increase! Raising all dollar wages and salaries can give the employees more purchasing power only if other consumers lose purchasing power. Those other consumers are people living on savings and fixed incomes—notably retirees. Since the pay increase had little effect on real wages and salaries, we should not be surprised that real profits did not change much either—that dollar profits rose with inflation.

What was the sequence of events that caused a rise in dollar wages to increase profits? And why did profits rise not 9% like prices, nor 10%, like wages, but 13%? To find the answers, we examine the effect of the pay raise on the profit sources.

When pay rates were increased in B-land, the wages of the capital-goods sector of course rose 10%. These wages are the largest source of profits of the consumer-goods sector. They are also a negative source of profits of the capital-goods sector. *Capital-goods-sector wages were $33 billion in B-land, compared to $30 billion in A-land.*

Because of inflation, expenditures for fixed investment, the primary source of profits of the capital-goods sector, were also higher in B-land than A-land. *Fixed investment was $49.1 billion in B-land, and $45.0 billion in A-land.*

Personal saving was also larger in B-land. The saving rate was the same in both countries, but personal income was 9% greater in B-land. *Thus, personal saving, a negative source of profits of the consumer-goods sector, was $10.9 billion in B-land but only $10 billion in A-land.*

Net foreign investment was not a contributor to profits in either country, because both countries had a zero balance of current accounts payments. The balances were zero for both capital- and consumer-goods sectors.

In both A-land and B-land, inventories expanded during the year. The additions to these stocks were *physically* equivalent in the two nations—that is, the same numbers and kinds of items were accumulated. But the dollar values placed on these additions were not the same. After contending with LIFO, FIFO, and other methods of inventory bookkeeping, *the accountants finally determined that the change in inventories of the consumer-goods sector in B-land was $3.3 billion, as compared to $3.0 billion. The inventories of the capital-goods sector rose $1.1 billion and $1.0 billion in B-land and A-land, respectively.*

Capital consumption allowances were not so different in the two countries. Depreciation and other charges accounted for by these allowances were based on the purchase prices of businesses' capital goods. Most of the capital goods owned by the consumer-goods sector during 19xx were bought in previous years. Only a small, but significant, part of consumer-goods-sector depreciation was based on newer, inflated prices of capital goods. *Thus, the capital consumption allowances of the consumer-goods sector were only slightly higher in B-land than in A-land, $15.3 billion compared to $15.0. For the capital-goods sector, capital consumption allowances were $5.1 billion in B-land and $5.0 billion in A-land.*

The government sector's surplus or deficit depends, of course, on all its receipts and expenditures. Revenues come from personal income, corporate profits, sales, real estate, gift and estate, and other taxes. In 19xx, inflation in B-land affected various types of government revenues unevenly. For example, the 10% pay rise promoted many B-landers into higher brackets, so income-tax collections rose 12% more than in A-land. On the other hand, receipts from gift, estate, and real-estate taxes and from license and other fees were only a little bit higher in B-land. The overall result was that by the fourth quarter of 19xx, B-land's government-sector revenues were running 9% higher than those in A-land.

We reported earlier that government outlays in B-land compared to A-land were up 10% for wages and 9% for social insurance and welfare payments. Purchases of goods and services from the business sector rose 9%. Interest payments on government's outstanding obligations did not increase, but those on newly issued bonds, notes, and bills rose, often quite rapidly, in response to inflation. Total government-sector expenditures before the end of 19xx were running 9% higher than in A-land.

Because both receipts and outlays were up 9%, *the government-sector deficit in B-land was 9% larger than in A-land, approximately $3.3 billion compared to $3.0 billion.*

Part of the increase in the B-land government-sector revenue came from rising corporate-profits tax receipts. Profits tax and dividends, the only profits sources still to be discussed, both follow the trend of profits. Since the B-land wage hike increased the net flow of profits from the other sources, profits tax and dividends also rose.

*The profits tax increased in proportion to profits because the tax* *rate was the same in A-land as in B-land. Corporate profits tax was $11.3 billion in B-land, compared to $10.0 billion in A-land.*

Finally, dividends follow the trend of profits but are less volatile and usually lag behind increases in profits. However, by the fourth quarter of 19xx, corporate boards of directors were raising dividends on common shares in B-land. Preferred stock dividends, which are almost always fixed, were unchanged. *Total dividends rose to $6.3 billion compared to $6.0 billion in A-land.*

Totaling the profit sources for each sector in each country, we arrived at the results shown in the following table.

| Consumer-Goods-Sector Sources of Profits* | A-land | B-land |
|---|---|---|
| capital-goods-sector wages | $30.0 billion | $33.0 billion |
| personal saving | −10.0 | −10.9 |
| net foreign investment | 0.0 | 0.0 |
| change in inventory | 3.0 | 3.3 |
| capital consumption allowances | −15.0 | −15.3 |
| dividends | 6.0 | 6.3 |
| government surplus (−), deficit (+) | 3.0 | 3.3 |
| corporate profits tax | 10.0 | 11.3 |
| profits before tax | $27.0 | $31.0 |

| Capital-Goods-Sector Sources of Profits* | | |
|---|---|---|
| fixed investment | 45.0 | 49.1 |
| capital-goods-sector wages | −30.0 | −33.0 |
| change in inventory | 1.0 | 1.1 |
| net foreign investment | 0 | 0 |
| capital consumption allowances | − 5.0 | − 5.1 |
| profits before tax | 11.0 | 12.1 |

And the grand totals:

| Total Business-Sector Profits, 19xx ($ billions) | A-land | B-land |
|---|---|---|
| Consumer-Goods Sector | $27.0 | $31.0 |
| Capital-Goods Sector | 11.0 | 12.1 |
| | $38.0 | $43.0 |
| Percentage difference, B-land compared to A-land | | +13.4% |

* In this chapter, as in chapter 5, we use abbreviated lists of the profit sources of the consumer- and capital-goods sectors, as explained in the notes at the end of the book. While these simplifications shorten our task, they do not affect the list of profit sources of the entire business sector. We would arrive at the same result in this chapter if our analysis were more detailed.

When accountants read the computer printout of the above table, they were astounded. By the fourth quarter of 19xx, *the 10% pay increase had caused total business profits to be 13.4% higher in B-land than in A-land!*

Where 10% more profits came from is easy to see, although the additional 3.4% may be puzzling. Giving workers more dollars to spend without increasing the available goods and services inevitably leads to a devaluation of the currency. Because of the way money flows from one sector of the economy to another, the inflation affected virtually all transactions. The profit sources were not excluded; they, too, rose.

The increase was 13.4% rather than 10% because the economy's reaction to the pay raise was not completed by the end of 19xx. In particular, capital consumption allowances failed to keep pace with inflation. Every other source of profits was inflated by at least 9%, but capital consumption allowances, a *negative* source of profits, was barely affected.

If no change in pay scales occurred after 19xx, capital consumption allowances would have gradually risen as much as the other profit sources. These expenses rise much more slowly than, for example, wages, because they are based on prices paid for capital goods, which were often purchased years earlier. (Depreciation charges under conventional accounting methods are based on the original purchase price of a capital good. Many accounting authorities recommend that these methods be changed to increase depreciation allowances along with capital-goods prices. The Department of Commerce has been making such adjustments in order to provide an alternative calculation of profits.)

Capital consumption allowances were not the only economic quantity that would take more than a year to adjust to inflation. Long-term interest rates are another example. *If no other pay increase occurred in B-land, eventually inflation would have raised all prices, costs, and payments 10%, the amount of the original pay increase. All the profit sources would then be 10% higher than in A-land.*

What does this fantasy have to do with the real world? Everything; it is not really fantasy.

B-land is an actual nation—or, rather, any one of a number of nations. It is the United States, France, or the United Kingdom in a recent year. Of course, the statistics we used are not those of any specific country, but they are realistic examples. We faithfully represented the basic process by which the economy generated higher profits in response to higher wages and salaries.

The greatest liberty we took was in the nature of the pay raise. In the United States, no good fairy magically increased wages by 10% on January 2 of any year. But American workers did receive average pay increases of 7%, 8%, or 9% from 1975 through 1980. Unlike the pay hikes brought on by the good fairy's spell, the raises in the United States were not uniform; some workers received none, others enormous ones.

Many of the other assumptions were, if not precisely similar to what happened in America, not far off the mark. For example, we assumed that the saving rate did not change, that people saved the same percentage of their incomes before and after the pay increases. The American personal-saving rate was 5.8% in 1950, 5.6% in 1960, 8.0% in 1970, and 5.7% in 1980. While the variations in this rate are sometimes considerable for a variety of reasons, the long-term trend seems to be reasonably flat.

The government sector's surplus or deficit is influenced by the phases of the business cycle, changes in unemployment, decisions about the programs it wants to support and how much it wants to pay for them, and by its willingness to levy taxes. Inflation has relatively little to do with the deficit or surplus. It affects government's receipts and expenditures without discrimination. Thus, more inflation means both larger receipts and larger expenditures.

Government-sector deficits have occurred when prices were stable, and surpluses have been recorded when inflation was rampant. For example, during 1964, the consumer price index rose 1.2% while there was a government-sector (federal, state, and local governments) deficit of $2.3 billion, but in 1979, when the CPI was advancing 13.3%, there was a surplus of $11.9 billion.

Although the United States' net foreign investment is never in perfect balance, our assumption that it was zero in B-land was not a serious departure from reality. Net foreign investment is usually a relatively small and insignificant source of profits. Moreover, a change in the American rate of inflation has a tendency to cause proportional changes in both our international current payments and receipts and, therefore, in the net foreign investment. But this source of profits is subject to countless influences from every part of the world. Our assumption above—that inflation did not significantly influence the surplus or deficit, and that this surplus or deficit had no influence on profits—was reasonable.

We also assumed that business, consumers, and government adopted a "business as usual" attitude, whereas it seems likely that business might panic if confronted with a sudden nationwide increase in labor costs of 10%. Yet, in the United States since 1970, rising labor costs have been accepted as an irksome and troublesome fact of life, but not a reason for panic. Indeed, during the last decade, pay raises were so regular and so large, and inflation so ongoing, that the economy became accustomed to adjusting. When a company's labor costs rose, it often increased prices almost immediately, knowing that these price boosts would be accepted in the inflationary environment.

In brief, we adopted assumptions that made our story easier to tell, but we did not misrepresent the process by which rising wages increase profits—and prices.

As for A-land, it is what B-land could have been had it not been plagued by inflationary pay increases. Workers were about as well off in A-land, although active workers in B-land did have a slight gain in real income (less than 1%)—at the expense of retirees and others living on savings, the victims of inflation. Next time the good fairy wants to raise the workers' standard of living, she should try a spell that increases the productivity of every worker 10%. Then everyone would enjoy a larger slice of economic pie.

Although pay increases can certainly be inflationary, the problem of spiraling prices can have more than one cause. Inflation in 1966, for example, had different causes than inflation in 1980. Nev-

ertheless, we have seen the workings of a key inflationary mecha-
nism. Rising labor costs have had far more responsibility for chronic
American inflation during the Seventies and early Eighties than any
of the popular scapegoats.

### EPILOGUE TO CHAPTER 6 FOR REVOLUTIONARIES

The foregoing refutations of three myths expose the fallacies of
those who believe in a profitless society. Profits, as we have seen,
cannot possibly be eliminated by expunging greed from the management of industry and commerce, instituting socialism, or grant-
ing enormous pay increases to the proletariat. Yet the profitless society is pursued, often violently, by many individuals.

There is a way for revolutionaries to eliminate profits, at least
long enough to destroy the system. They need only persuade the
proletariat to save 15% more of their incomes than currently. Selling
this plan would be a formidable task for the leaders of the revolution, but they would receive help from many staunch capitalists who
would applaud the proposal to increase saving as "sound economics."

To maintain discipline, the revolutionaries would have to be vig-
ilant. They could not tolerate any backsliding—no depositing $35
with one teller and then going to another window to borrow $50.
The workers would have to increase their *net* saving by 15% of their
incomes.

Since personal saving is a negative source of profits, the capitalists would discover almost immediately that they were unable to sell
their goods and services at a profit. By increasing saving, the proletariat could remove the oxygen of capitalism—profits would be
eliminated.

# 7

# The Profit Incentive

The amount of profits flowing into the business sector is vital to the success of a capitalist economy. Equally crucial is how these profits are divided among the country's firms. For capitalism to serve a society well, profits must be distributed in a way that motivates investors to sponsor efficient production of desired goods and services.

Microeconomics, the branch of economics concerned with the behavior of individual enterprises and industries, explains how competition and markets influence investors. The essentials of microeconomic theory are not controversial, and our conclusions about markets and competition are no different from those of other economists. But our approach to the subject enables us to relate the profits of individual firms and industries to the aggregate flow of profits from their sources. Later, we will see that this relationship explains how the flow of aggregate profits affects the output of firms, the nation's prosperity, employment, and so forth.

Before continuing our examination of the working of a capitalist system, we should note that no nation is purely capitalist. The United States, which is about as capitalist as any, still leaves such functions as mail delivery, highway maintenance, subway and some railroad transportation, and even some sales of alcoholic beverages to government. Much larger portions of the economies of most European countries are owned and operated by government or government-owned corporations. State-owned broadcasting facilities, utilities, and public transportation systems are the rule. Some of the governments of these countries even operate steel, automobile, and other manufacturing facilities. Still, we consider them capitalist because their economies are primarily dependent on the markets, competition, and profit incentives that we discuss in this chapter.

Free-enterprise economists from Adam Smith to present-day scholars have celebrated capitalism's success at putting self-interest, or acquisitiveness, to good use. Investors get special credit for the unlikely virtue of greed. Their zeal in pursuing profits has been praised for making capitalism a system that serves workers and consumers—and investors—better than any other.

When Adam Smith referred to self-interest, he did not mean rapaciousness, a greed that infects a person's perception of right and wrong and leads him to break laws, lie, and disregard the rights of others. Rather, he meant ambition to acquire wealth and enjoy leisure, a kind of greed that is certainly selfish but does not destroy an individual's respect for the law or fair play. The greedy investor who represents the capitalist ideal may not feel responsible for the lot of his fellow human beings, but he will not steal from them.

The role of the investor in a capitalist system is, of course, to finance production and employment. (An investor is anyone who contributes to the financing of a profit-seeking enterprise. Included are proprietors who invest directly in their own businesses and owners of stocks, bonds, and other financial instruments.) An investor who puts his money on the line enables business to buy capital and inventory goods, compensate employees, and pay other expenses. He expects, or at least hopes, that the activities made possible by his investment will bring him profits. When the system is working properly, he will get those profits only if his company efficiently produces goods and services that society wants.

Investors are motivated primarily by the prospect of increasing their wealth. Certainly, there are exceptions. An investor with a large income may seek an investment that will, over the short term, incur losses and thereby reduce his taxes. Or someone fascinated with the idea of owning a magazine or baseball team may invest in such a venture even though the profit outlook is not promising. A person may finance a theatrical production in order to give the leading role to a friend. Generally, however, only financial considerations are on the investor's mind: how much he is likely to gain, the risks, and so forth.

When it comes to evaluating a potential investment, the investor is similar to the bettor at the track. The smaller the likelihood of the horse winning, the greater the odds must be before the bettor will venture his money. The investor, too, weighs his risks against the potential payoff, or profit. The potential reward for financing a long shot must be many times greater than the amount risked before the investment is worthwhile. And, again like the horseplayer, the investor requires relatively little incentive to persuade him to finance a "sure thing."

The odds that the gambler reads on the board at the track may be 7-to-5, 8-to-1, or 20-to-1. Usually an investor must make his own calculation of what an investment might bring him. His potential reward is measured by his estimated *return on investment* (ROI). ROI is simply the gain or profit, as a percentage of the amount invested, usually expressed as an annual rate. (Suppose Maria Garibaldi had $100,000 invested in a restaurant that served marvelous pizza. Last year her profit was $30,000, so her ROI was 30%.)

Of course, the investor's decision is more complicated than the gambler's, partly because many degrees of business success and failure are possible. Still, the fundamental question for both of them is: will the reward for success be big enough to outweigh the risks of failure?

Society has criteria for evaluating investments, too. It wants them to put people to work efficiently producing desired goods and services. Members of society enjoy the highest standard of living when business hires the greatest possible number of workers, uses them most efficiently, and produces the goods and services that consumers most want.

Since the economy only generates a finite amount of profits, society wants every dollar of profit to lead to as much employment and production as possible. In healthy economies, a relatively small profit will usually motivate a large volume of output. However, in some economies, a few investors may manage to collect most of the available profits while financing only a small volume of production. The meager amount of profits remaining does not motivate other investors to sponsor much additional output. These economies produce much less than they should.

From society's point of view, when a firm obtains $1 of sales revenue, almost all of that dollar should pay for labor, purchases of inventories, and other things needed for production. Society should not give investors 95¢ of profit for financing 5¢ worth of production. When *profit margins* are as small as possible, society is getting the maximum production and employment out of its investors.

Profit margins, like return on investment, are a way of measuring profitability. Whereas ROI is profits as a percentage of *investment,* a profit margin is profits as a percentage of *sales* (and other) *revenue.* For any firm, the two measures tend to rise and fall together, but each relates profits to a different aspect of the business. (For example, Maria Garibaldi sold $300,000 worth of pizza and other delectable foods last year. Her profit, we recall, was $30,000, so her profit margin was 10%. The 10% tells us how well Ms. Garibaldi fared on her average sale. The ROI, which was 30%, tells us how well she did with her investment.)

We will discuss profitability in terms of profit margins because we are interested in the economy from the point of view of society. We want to know how profits affect employment, production, and the standard of living. Profit margins are also a component of prices, and therefore important when discussing inflation.

For any business enterprise with a particular product, sales volume, and method of operation, there is a profit margin that is, from society's standpoint, ideal. Society wants profit margins to be low—to assure a maximum amount of production for the profits available—but it does not want margins to fall too far. If profitability were too low, investors would not support a great many useful enterprises. Many companies would shut down. Moreover, investors would not be willing to take new risks, to sponsor research or innovation. From society's point of view, optimum profit margins are generally the smallest possible ones that can still satisfy investors.

Naturally, no single profit margin is optimum for every business, or even for one business under all circumstances. What is a desirable profit margin is affected by a firm's cost structure, expectations about the future of the industry, inventory turnover, and a host of other considerations. A supermarket that turns over its inventory 14 times a year does not need margins as high as those required by a gift shop that turns its stock over only twice a year. A discount department store is delighted with profit margins that would be a disaster for a machine shop. An investor might turn down an offer to buy a gasoline service station in the south Bronx even though he would invest in a similar station with an identical profit margin in Honesdale, Pennsylvania, where the risk of loss from crime is lower. Executives, accountants, and others familiar with an industry have fairly precise ideas of the margins that a firm in that industry needs in order to be satisfactorily profitable.

If every firm in an industry were virtually identical, the optimum profit margin for each, in society's view, would be the same. However, in most industries, some firms are more efficient than others, some offer better products, and not all of them have the same costs. Society should encourage those that serve it best, those that use human and material resources efficiently and produce desired goods and services. It should give less encouragement to mediocre companies that waste resources or produce inferior products. Society should give the superior companies an incentive to expand and put the inferior ones under pressure to improve or get out of the business.

Therefore, society is best served when especially effective firms are able to secure profit margins above the bare minimum required by their investors, and when less adept enterprises are unable to obtain satisfactory profits. This situation will motivate investors to support superior firms and upgrade or abandon inferior ones. Only if all the firms in the industry are closely competitive will society want to reward them all with more or less the same profit margin.

Thus, although optimum profit margins are generally the lowest possible that are acceptable to investors, the margins that society considers optimum for some firms are more or less than these minimum levels. The variations in profit margins from firm to firm within an industry serve society by inducing investors to determine which shall survive and which shall be eliminated through a process of "natural selection."

Not every firm has a positive optimum profit margin—some firms should secure no profits. Society does not want to give any profits to companies that waste great amounts of manpower and natural resources producing goods that its competitors can turn out far more efficiently. Nor does it want profits to go to firms that manufacture items that nobody wants. Society certainly does not want to give profits to enterprises that provide illegal goods or services such as pipe bombs or arson. Optimally, all these enterprises should not profit at all; investors should not be tempted to finance such activities.

Fortunately, a force prevails that generally prevents profit margins from becoming either excessive or inadequate. It is competition. Through a chain of events described in great detail in any microeconomics textbook, competition adjusts market prices and therefore largely determines profit margins.

Market prices tend to create a balance between what buyers want to buy and what sellers want to sell. In the language of academic economics, the market price is the price at which the quantity demanded equals the quantity supplied. In everyday English, this statement means that the price will not stay so high that buyers are discouraged from purchasing as much as sellers offer for sale. Gluts will not exist, at least not for long. And prices will not remain so low that more buyers are flocking to the market than the sellers will accommodate.

Because of the market's actions, buyers in capitalist countries can usually find what they want to purchase, although they may not want or be able to buy it at the offered price. In the Soviet Union, by contrast, consumers with bulging wallets are frequently unable to buy goods and services that they would love to have—even by paying more than the stated prices—because the products are simply unavailable. Robert G. Kaiser, in his 1976 book, *Russia,* reports that "people buy and eat what is available. Russians carry string bags with them at all times, in purse or pocket. They're known as 'just in case' bags, for use in case one happens across a desirable product for sale on the daily rounds." Soviet officials set prices without paying much attention to whether the quantity supplied balances the quantity demanded.

Under capitalism, competition maintains the prices that produce these balances. Should a change occur in the buyers' demand for a product or the sellers' willingness or ability to supply it, competition alters prices to restore the balance. If a price is too high, buyers become discouraged, and eager vendors are unable to sell as much as they had expected. Competition intensifies. Firms try to win more customers by shaving their prices. Prices fall until buyers are induced to purchase all of the product that business is selling.

You see this phenomenon every year when the Christmas-shopping season draws to a close. Almost overnight, the demand for thousands of consumer items falls. Competition to sell them intensifies; *everything* seems to be on sale; many prices plunge. Prices also adjust when the supply of a product changes. When orange growers enjoy especially bountiful crops, and oranges pour into supermarkets and grocery stores, the price of this fruit begins to drop in response to the increasingly competitive environment. Prices decrease until consumers are induced to buy enough oranges to prevent them from rotting in the bins.

The example of the bumper orange crop illustrates how competition forces excessive prices down until a balance exists between the quantity customers wish to purchase and the quantity sellers provide. But what would happen if prices were *below* the level at which this balance exists? The bins would contain the same quantity of oranges, but the fruit would be so cheap—a great bargain—that consumers would be eager to buy more than usual. Stores would rapidly run out. Orange-lovers would have to plan their shopping expeditions to coincide with the arrival of new shipments if they wanted to continue to enjoy freshly squeezed juice every morning.

Situations like the one just described are rare in capitalist economies because markets almost always adjust prices so rapidly that potential shortages are nipped in the bud. When customers begin to have the slightest difficulty obtaining a product, competition among sellers becomes lax. Sellers can and do raise prices. Prices rise to the point where buyers are discouraged from purchasing any more than firms are willing or able to sell. Equilibrium—the balance between demand and supply—is restored.

Occasionally, markets do not respond so quickly, and customers encounter scarcities. Few American operators of motor vehicles can forget what happened in 1974 and 1979 when events in the Middle East created gasoline shortages. Lines that sometimes stretched for miles appeared at the pumps. To say that competition among gasoline vendors was weak is an understatement. After the 1979 episode, when controls were lifted and prices were free to rise in response to market pressures, competition revived. The quantity demanded once again equaled the quantity supplied. Gas stations that had closed early ever since 1974 were again keeping long hours in order to pick up additional sales, and were even cheerfully cleaning windshields.

Almost anyone who has ever entered a supermarket or gasoline station is familiar with how competition sets prices. Do these market prices necessarily give firms optimal profit margins? No. But competition leads business to make other adjustments that do tend to assure that profit margins are neither too wide nor too narrow.

When investors and the managers they employ decide what their firms should produce in order to respond to competitive conditions, their decisions serve society in two ways. First, although businessmen try to maximize their profits, the aggregate effect of their actions tends to be optimum profit margins. Second, the most desired goods and services are produced. Both of these favorable outcomes result from a continuous process—the expansion of some industries and the contraction of others.

Consider an industry in which the market price is *high*—where, in other words, profit margins are *excessive*. Customers are paying an excessive price for the product, a premium above what it would cost a company to provide it and obtain an optimum profit. This willingness on the part of buyers is an indication that the product is one that they want badly. Society would like the economy to produce more of it. Thanks to competition, it will.

Or, rather, thanks to a lack of competition. With so many willing customers paying high prices and buying everything the firms in the industry produce, competition among sellers is clearly lax. Investors are likely to finance new firms to compete in the industry in order to take advantage of the opportunity for high profits. Other investors are willing to finance expansions of firms already in the market so that they may enjoy even higher sales, and thus more profits. As the industry's capacity increases, so does the supply of the product. Competition intensifies. Prices fall. Eventually, the profit margins are reduced to optimum levels. An incentive for firms to expand no longer exists.

Electronics industries expanded rapidly in the latter part of the twentieth century with the expectation of large profits. Technological breakthroughs that enabled business to introduce minicomputers, pocket calculators, home computers, and digital watches often led to high profits for the firms that pioneered these products. Other firms therefore decided to enter these markets. The supplies increased; competition rapidly became keen; prices declined. After a while, the profit margins on many of these products became more or less optimum.

Another well-known example of expansion occurred in the hosiery industry. The firms that introduced pantyhose enjoyed high profit margins. Wall Street was enthusiastic about their stocks. More and more companies sought to share in the pantyhose bonanza. Soon, competition became a strong force acting to reduce prices. Since that time, Wall Street analysts have barely mentioned pantyhose.

On the other hand, when the market price is *too low,* when profit margins are *below* optimum levels, customers are buying the product only at an unreasonably low price. The low value of the product to buyers indicates that the industry is producing too much—more than society wants. Competition will cause the industry to shrink. When firms in an industry find that competition is too severe for them to obtain acceptable returns, they are forced to make changes. Some companies may redirect their efforts—produce less of the unprofitable item and more of other goods or services. Other firms may shut down their least efficient plants, or even go out of business entirely. Eventually, the supply of the unprofitable product shrinks enough so that competition is no longer too severe. The prices rise until profit margins are restored to optimum levels.

Diaper services, which flourished during the post–World War II baby boom, are a good example of an industry that contracted in the face of overwhelming competition among sellers. The sharp decline in the birthrate in the 1960s and the introduction of disposable diapers almost obliterated the industry. Only a remnant survives.

A change in profit margins that induces an industry either to expand or contract is a manifestation of a change in that industry's total profits. Thus, the industry's total profits eventually determine its volume of production, the number of people it employs, and the amount of its investment in plant and equipment. In other words, the portion of the economy's total flow of profits secured by the firms in a particular business ultimately determines how large their industry will be.

This amount of profits depends on two phenomena, one of which is competition. Industries, like individual companies, vie for profits. For example, during the 1950s, '60s and '70s, trucking companies were hauling increasing quantities of freight, often at the expense of railroads. Because of lower costs, door-to-door deliveries, and other advantages, truckers won profits away from railroads. Consequently, trucking companies expanded while rail service shrank, and railroad employment declined.

The second and no less important phenomenon determining the amount of profits that an industry secures is the size of the economy's total flow of profits. Regardless of how competition distributes profits among firms, virtually every industry will benefit when aggregate profits rise and suffer when they fall. When we examine the problem of unemployment, we will focus on how changes in the flow of profits lead to the expansion or contraction of industries throughout the business sector.

Sometimes a firm continually achieves profit margins that are larger than necessary to meet investors' minimum requirements. Year after year, it outperforms its competition hands-down. For many years, no cameramaker produced an instant camera to compete with Polaroid's. McDonald's hamburger restaurants became a ubiquitous feature of the American landscape because of unmatched efficiency. When Federal Express became well established, its overnight package-delivery service was apparently so much more efficient than its competitors' that it enjoyed enviable profitability.

The great rewards obtained by companies such as these are not necessarily excessive. Huge profits serve society as an inducement to firms to become pioneers and innovators, to improve their contributions to the economy. As long as star companies enjoy especially wide profit margins, competitors have an incentive to try to match their superior products or methods. Thanks to profits, businesses in a healthy capitalist economy constantly try to outdo each other, break old records, and increasingly satisfy consumer desires. The chance of gaining large profits motivates investors to seek progress. Thus, competition constantly keeps the economy changing to better serve society.

Unfortunately, competition is not perfect. Many obstacles to the proper functioning of markets exist. Buyers often have less than complete information about offerings and prices, and, as a result, they may respond slowly to price changes, quality improvements, and new product introductions. Free markets are compromised by monopolies and by some industries consisting of only a few, very large firms. Governments, too, sometimes distort competition. Some regulations shield companies from competition or limit their ability to offer good products at favorable prices. (Of course, governments often have valid reasons to interfere with markets. Society does not want hand grenades to be sold in sporting-goods stores.)

Some of the greatest damage to free markets in the United States and some other countries has been inflicted by government when it has decided to act on the notion that tight money is good for the economy. When government makes loans artificially difficult to secure and interest rates artificially high, competition is hampered in its role as an economic manager. Lenders in a free-market economy are supposed to demand a return commensurate with their evaluations of the risks they incur. If the Friendly Bank loans money to the Apple-Banana Company, its interest rate should be based on its appraisal of the risk that the loan will not be repaid. But once government creates a scarcity of lendable funds, the interest rate reflects the imposed shortage of credit, not just the bank's risks.

The slump in housing that began in 1979 did not have much to do with a sudden decline in the need for dwellings. It had a great deal to do with a marketplace that was grotesquely distorted by high interest rates created by the Federal Reserve—not by lenders reappraising the risks involved in lending funds to consumers.

Even when nothing interferes with competition, the economy may be slow to respond to changes in market conditions, because companies have great difficulty entering and leaving certain industries. Seldom does one hear of a new domestic firm in an industry that requires a huge capital investment, such as railroad transportation, auto manufacturing, or integrated aluminum production. Existing firms in such industries may operate at a loss for a seemingly indefinite period because of the enormous sums tied up in investments that are not easily abandoned. Furthermore, political and other factors may come into play. Chrysler was bailed out by government loan guarantees, partly because of political pressure exerted by groups trying to preserve the jobs of its employees and those of its suppliers.

Undoubtedly, we cannot always depend on competition to optimize profit margins. Nevertheless, it usually does a pretty good job. Perfect competition may not be achievable, but competition in the United States is sufficiently healthy to make the system work more or less the way it is supposed to. Some markets, like the coffee-shop market in New York City, come quite close to the theoretical ideal. Others, like the electric utility industry, do not. Still, most American businesses are constantly occupied with the necessity of competing, directly or indirectly, with other firms.

Part of the reason for the historical success of capitalism in the United States is that the government has usually supported and defended the system. Although Uncle Sam has sometimes acted unwisely or unjustly, he has done a reasonably good job in maintaining fair competition through the administration of antitrust acts, securities laws, truth-in-advertising regulations, and so forth. Government successfully limits monopoly power, along with market conspiracy, collusion, and other undesirable practices. It has the critical, continuing task of policing the economy against unlawful practices without itself becoming a source of undesirable interference.

But does healthy competition necessarily mean a healthy economy? Even if capitalism is working properly, is it a good system? Is it better than socialism—or any other system? Is capitalism just?

# 8

# Capitalism and Justice

Critics of capitalism have insisted that it is an inherently unjust system. Their assertion is based primarily on the belief that investors take a large slice of the economic pie and give nothing in return. This notion is so pervasive that even many capitalists give it some credence. When capitalism is assailed for its alleged injustice, these people often duck the ethical issue and defend the system on the basis of its efficiency and productivity.

Yet capitalism does have a fundamental principle of justice: the nation's income should be distributed to individuals in accordance with their contributions to production. Whenever a capitalist system is working properly, this principle is upheld.

One rationale for the "reward based on contribution" concept of economic justice is that it preserves the "natural" relationship between output and material reward. Since prehistoric times, a lone man, family, tribe, or independent social unit of any size has always found that its income is equal to its production.

Members of many capitalist societies find this version of economic ethics quite satisfactory for all those who are able to be productive. Americans agree that we would like people to be rewarded on this basis, except individuals who are disabled, ill, or otherwise unable to support themselves. We are willing to be taxed in order to pay for the maintenance of those who could not otherwise survive. True, we may argue over who deserves how much, who is truly in need of government support, or why a ne'er-do-well who inherited

$2 million should be allowed to be a playboy. Nevertheless, our ideological consensus is generally strong.

When a capitalist system is working properly, it adheres reasonably well to its basic ethic. Workers are generally paid according to how much society values their efforts, and investors are rewarded according to their contributions to production.

But *what* does an investor contribute to production that justifies his sometimes generous reward? After all, most people earn their living by performing tasks that, either directly or indirectly, provide goods and services of value to our population. Why should investors be able to obtain income by simply gambling with their money in an economic game that seems to provide for many more winners than losers? (Of course, an investor may be—and in the United States usually is—a worker. When we discuss investors and workers as if they were distinct individuals, we are really talking about people in their roles as investors and people in their roles as workers. Recall that we have defined "worker" to include anyone who is compensated for doing a job—a top executive, a menial laborer, or someone in between.)

An investor contributes to production by employing workers, including managers; paying for their materials and equipment; and bearing risks. He studies markets and makes decisions that enable them to allocate the nation's resources. Do these actions constitute a contribution to production that deserves a reward? Yes; the investor gives something to society, something that greatly facilitates production, something that he provides at a real cost to himself.

Most people are skeptical of this justification of the investor's rewards, because they tend to neglect, or at least inadequately emphasize, one essential, fundamental aspect of the investor-employee relationship: the role of risk transference in employment. They take for granted that having a job is simply trading work for money, and overlook an invisible service that investors provide when employing workers—insurance.

Production always involves risks. Before we discuss the insurance furnished by employers, we will examine the nature of the risks that they assume.

Economic risks are inevitable. Chance plays games not only with health, happiness, and horse races, but with productive activities like growing potatoes, selling hot dogs, and building a house. We have no guarantee that any of our efforts will be rewarded. Even Robinson Crusoe, in his simple, one-man economy, was burdened by production risks—the possibilities of work being to no avail, of tools lost or broken, or of crops destroyed. He once tried to make a barrel, but "I could never make a cask to be hooped . . .," he wrote in his journal, "though I spent many weeks about it; I could neither put in the heads, or joint the staves so true to one another, as to make them hold water; so I gave that also over." These weeks, during which he might have built a chair or woven a basket, were time entirely lost.

Crusoe once made a canoe—an enormous undertaking—only to learn that he could not budge the hulking vessel, let alone launch it. His first corn crop was another failure. Perhaps he could have reduced some of his risks if he had been more careful or clever, but they were largely inevitable.

A more populous, complicated economy also has risks. Crops still fail; plastics, metals, and other materials turn out to be substandard; manufactured goods prove to be faulty; factories catch fire; workers are injured; machines break down; scarcities of raw materials force shutdowns; and a variety of other misfortunes occur. Also present in large economies is a class of economic risk that our involuntary hermit did not have to contend with: marketing risks. The safe, efficient completion of a product does not mean that the manufacturer will not sustain a loss. Perhaps consumers will never hear about the product, or they may not be willing to buy enough of it. People may not be interested in purchasing the product at a price that covers the costs of manufacturing and distributing it, or they may not want it at any price.

Marketing risks arise from the uncertainties inherent in a specialized economy where people perform different tasks and depend on one another for fulfillment of their needs. A manufacturer cannot read the minds of the entire population. How many blue dress shirts the nation will want is uncertain. The number of snow shovels will depend on the weather.

If we lived in a society devoid of change, marketing risks would be much smaller. There would be little question about what would be consumed. However, new products, better production methods, and freedom of choice for consumers greatly increase the chances of making unwanted products, being priced out of a market, or having an inventory become obsolete. Thus, marketing risks are much greater in Western Europe than behind the Iron Curtain. Given progress, change, and a broad selection of most consumer goods, marketing risks, like production risks, are inevitable.

These economic risks are often great burdens to individuals who bear them. For example, Sam, the proprietor of a one-man tailor shop on Main Street, does not sleep well. He confides to his wife that he has nightmares in which calamities befall his little business, the enterprise in which he has invested almost every spare cent he has ever had. Sometimes he dreams of a plague of moths descending upon his wool inventory. On other nights, he envisions a shop opening right next door, manned by robots that produce twelve top-quality suits an hour and sell them at bargain prices. Or he dreams that the three-piece suit is considered gauche in executive suites and that jeans with a flannel shirt are *de rigueur.* Although Sam's wife knows that his fears are exaggerated, she, too, worries because she understands that there are real risks of serious losses that would bring hardship if not disaster.

But suppose that Donald, a well-to-do customer, makes Sam an offer. He has long been impressed with the quality of the tailor's work and wants to buy his business. Sam would continue to run the shop, but instead of earning whatever came in, he would receive a fixed salary. For doing exactly the same work, he would be guaranteed payment. Under the new arrangement, if moths damaged inventories, it would be Donald's loss. If Sam's suits did not sell, it would be Donald's loss. At worst, the operation would fold and Sam would have to look for a new job. But his personal wealth would be intact and he would have been paid for all the work he had done.

Of course, Sam might prefer his independence, the status of owning his own business, or the chance of increasing his income, and therefore politely refuse. But if Donald does become Sam's employer, he will be providing a service for the tailor: work insurance.

He promises to protect his employee from the possibility that the latter's efforts will not be rewarded. By making the commitment, Donald assumes the risk himself.

In all fairness, Donald ought to receive some compensation for providing this service. Sam, by accepting a fixed sum of money as his salary, would relinquish to Donald any other funds that his efforts might bring. This chance of receiving additional money is Donald's remuneration for providing insurance. Donald accepts the risk of bearing Sam's loss and thus acquires a chance to profit. This insurance relationship is a fundamental aspect of employment.

Employment is similar to other kinds of insurance. When Sam purchases a policy for his house or his car, he transfers his risk to the insurance company. In return for protecting Sam against disasters at home or on the road, the company obtains the chance of making money. In the event that claims are less than the premiums it collects, the company profits. Both Donald and the insurance company agree to enter insurance relationships with Sam because they think that the odds favor their securing profits. They may lose, but they consider the gamble worth taking.

People frequently overlook the transfer of risk from employee to employer. Unlike Sam the tailor or Robinson Crusoe, they fail to realize that work has no inherent value. Sam learned from the experience of bearing business risks that, no matter how admirable and diligent his efforts, his work was worth no more than the value of what he produced. Robinson Crusoe realized that his weeks of exertion in a vain attempt to construct a cask were worth nothing.

Unlike Crusoe, an employee of a large organization, be he a steelworker or an executive of an automobile manufacturer, probably does not realize that his efforts may turn out to be of little or no value. An individual worker can believe that his personal contribution was valuable even though no one will buy the company's end products. Because he worked hard and applied all his skills, he is unwilling to accept the fact that his efforts turned out to be worth little. Therefore, he may fail to realize that his compensation is a certain, set amount only because his employer insures his work.

When the government employs, or insures the work of, all or

almost all of the labor force, the system is socialism. A socialist government does not have a financial risk. It may lose money on some of its enterprises, but it will more than recover those losses through its profitable operations. The government collects the profits simply because they are there, not because it needs or wants them.

Under socialism, the profits collected by the government cannot be used by any individual investors to purchase large helpings of economic pie at the workers' expense. Nevertheless, work insurance under socialism is not free. If a factory turns out 500,000 gloves with four fingers instead of five, if a ship sinks, or if a crop fails, who really bears the loss? Everyone. The government provides the money that covers the loss, but everyone in the nation suffers by receiving a smaller piece of pie. Workers do not really rid themselves of the risks associated with their labors, but instead share these risks with everyone else in the nation. Everyone shares in anyone's triumphs or mistakes.

In nations that are not primarily socialist but whose governments run enterprises, the entire society pays the costs of insuring the efforts of public employees. These socialized risks are often significant. The costs to the taxpayers of the inefficient government-supported automobile industry in Britain, steel industry in Italy, and telephone-communication industry in France are considerable. In these cases, citizens can see the costs to themselves in terms of pounds, lira, or francs if they know how much the government enterprises are losing. But socialized risks are borne by the people whether they are visible or not. Losses always represent subtractions from the economic pie.

When individual investors insure the work of most of the labor force, the system is capitalism. They, unlike a socialist government, are not assured profits. Even though American business has had aggregate profits every year since 1932, many firms—and their investors—have suffered losses. From the arid farms of the 1930s dust bowl to Polavision, the ill-fated instant movies from Polaroid, investors have suffered losses, moderate and enormous. All told, they have parted with many billions of dollars. Think of the onetime blue-chip Pennsylvania Railroad or the Ford Motor Company's Edsel. Also prominent on the list of financial disasters are W. T. Grant, whose stores stood alongside Woolworth's on the nation's main streets; Underwood, a name that was almost synonymous with "typewriter"; and Three-Mile Island, a power plant once identified with progress and success.

These ill-fated ventures emphasize why investors need to be offered an incentive—a reasonable chance of making attractive profits—before they will agree to insure the work of employees and purchase capital goods and materials for them to work with. Thus, profits in a private-enterprise economy, unlike those in a socialist system, encourage the assumption of risks. Under capitalism, the government does not collect and retain the profits, but allows investors to compete for them by insuring work and otherwise financing production.

When investors obtain profits, they can use these funds for purchasing some of the economic pie, thereby reducing the amount available to workers. Although investors generally do not spend all of their profits on personal consumption, their savings from profit income give them potential purchasing power, which they can draw on later.

Under socialism, employees need not give any pie to investors. Why should society permit any slice to be taken out of the pie? Why not "purchase cheaper insurance"—that is, adopt socialism?

*Because the capitalist brand of work insurance includes something that government insurance does not. Investors provide an extra service that results in the high efficiency and responsiveness to consumer wishes that distinguish successful capitalist economies.* This extra service comprises investors' scrutiny of investment opportunities, the selection of those projects that promise the best returns, and their efforts to assure the successful operation of their enterprises. Whether investors make these decisions themselves or hire others to manage their funds, they determine what will be produced and by which firms, what new ideas will be tried, and so on. In economies without investors, governments have to employ bureaucrats to make these decisions.

An obvious question is "Which way will workers enjoy more economic pie—if investors (and markets) plan the economy's activities, or if government employees handle the task?" Later we will look at the effectiveness of capitalism and socialism in practice.

Under capitalism, as well as under socialism, economic risks involve not just money but goods, services, health, and safety. In any system, less pie is available when misfortunes occur. When a capitalist enterprise fails to be profitable, it represents a waste or loss of society's resources *and* a loss of the investors' money. If the loss is enough to curtail these investors' personal-consumption expenditures, they suffer a greater loss of pie than do most members of society. Even if they can absorb the loss without reducing their own standard of living, their total wealth—their potential purchasing power—is diminished.

Thus, by taking risks and competing for profits, investors provide society with two valuable services: (1) they provide employment, and (2) they decide, partly through their managers, how to use the resources available to business. These are real contributions to the production process, even when provided by the greediest skinflint ever to drool over potential profits.

Until now, we have said that investors *win* profits, but have avoided the issue of whether they *earn* profits. Because investors *do* contribute to production, they may indeed earn profits. If the system is working properly, all profits will be earned.

But profits are not always earned. We have compared firms competing for profits to children competing for prizes in a school contest. If the contest is unfair or if some pupils cheat, the winners will not have earned their rewards. The same is true in the economic contest among firms. Or if the number of prizes available becomes excessive—if, for instance, the fourteenth runner-up in a 15-student spelling bee wins a set of encyclopedias—we have reason to doubt that the winners have really earned their prizes. Similarly, if the amount of profits in the economy is too great, the excess cannot be earned. Any profits above optimum margins (which may be very high in the case of an exceptional firm) are not earned.

As long as investors act within the law, the law properly protects the interests of society, and the optimum amount of profits is flowing into the economy, the role of the investor is consistent with the underlying ethic of capitalism.

But what about the person who sells stock short and makes a bundle overnight? Or the commodities speculator who makes a quick killing on cotton because of a false rumor about a new kind of cotton-eating caterpillar? Indeed, such income appears to be completely unrelated to any "insurance for work."

Actually, these *capital gains* are the result of the market activity in this country that allows investors to trade and sell risks to one another. Some win, some lose, but there is no overall effect on the amount of profits flowing through the economy. Speculating in financial markets benefits society to the extent it facilitates the flow of investment funds to where they are needed.

Earlier we showed that the traditional notion of a capitalist-worker class struggle is a destructive myth and that it is incompatible with the relationship of aggregate wages to profits in the broad economy. Now we have a new view of the employer-employee relationship—insurance—that is compatible with the wage-profit relationship. This fresh perspective helps us to understand something about making the system work well.

Employer and employee, whether they recognize it or not, are linked by a common interest. As many Japanese and some American companies have demonstrated, both insurer and insured benefit when risks are reduced. Individually, employers and employees may argue over the valuation of the work insured, but they have a mutual interest in avoiding losses. The insurer knows that losses come out of his own pocket, and the insured understands that they may eventually result in a lower valuation of his work (lower wages) or even the cancellation of his policy (job).

Some companies, especially in Japan, have gone so far as to offer workers an even more comprehensive type of policy. They guarantee not only that any work the employee performs will be rewarded, but also that he will have meaningful work available even if business slumps or his current job becomes obsolete.

Another arrangement is for employees to bear a small, yet meaningful, part of the risk arising from their work. They receive a bonus when the company does well and forgo this compensation when its profits fall. Such a bonus underscores the common interests of the worker and investor. It resembles the "deductible" portion of an insurance claim.

When employment is perceived as insurance for work, the idea of a class struggle between employers and employees no longer makes sense. "Arise ye insured, and overthrow the insurers!" is hardly an inspiring, revolutionary battle cry.

Unfortunately, the prevailing view is that employee and employer are seller and buyer of a commodity called "labor." According to traditional wisdom, workers sell their services in a market just as other vendors sell butter, diamonds, shoeshines, or railroad cars. There are many markets for labor: markets for executives, masons, editors, refrigerator repairmen, bodyguards, and so forth. Wages and salaries are set, it is claimed, just as prices are determined, according to the law of supply and demand.

However, labor markets differ in some respects from markets for the products of business. As we explained earlier, they are especially imperfect. Unions and professional associations may monopolize certain skills. Prejudice may unfairly handicap some "sellers of labor." In an isolated town with one big employer, the "buyer of labor" may exert undue influence over the market. Moreover, labor differs from most goods and services because it is bought not once but continually. For a buyer to change suppliers—that is, for a firm to replace an employee—is by no means a costless transaction. Finding and training a new person may cost more than the employee's annual salary. For a seller to change customers—that is, to leave one employer and take a job with another—may also be expensive. Locating a job may require a great deal of time, effort, and money. When transaction costs become this high, and often unpredictable, market mechanisms are seriously impeded.

Because of the peculiar characteristics of labor markets, comparing an employment agreement to the sale of a commodity—beef, for example—is ridiculous. Wages and salaries are not determined as simply as meat prices. An experienced operator of a highly specialized piece of equipment may pressure his boss for a raise by threatening to quit, an action that would force the employer to train an unskilled worker to replace him. But a rib roast never threatens to leave an oven, compelling the consumer to train a hamburger to take its place.

To discuss labor markets realistically, the insurance aspect of employment should be kept in mind. An insurance company can discuss different ways of managing risks with a client, and then agree on a policy, which remains in effect for a period of time. A commodity vendor simply sells an unchanging product—the transaction is consummated at a particular moment. Although neither metaphor completely describes the institution of employment, the insurance analogy produces images not of a transaction immediately completed but of a continuing, complex relationship involving risk transfer.

The "commodity" view of employment is less and less appropriate as our labor force becomes more specialized, technologically oriented, and highly trained. Such issues as job security, retraining, turnover, rank and file participation in problem-solving, and job satisfaction are becoming steadily more important to personnel management. The manager who thinks of his employees as commodities is not likely to be successful. The manager who *treats* his subordinates like commodities will usually fare even less well.

The companies that have taken the greatest strides toward conquering the class-struggle myth and raising productivity do not look on their employees as commodities but as complex, valuable resources—and, most important, as *human* resources. Workers at one of these firms may not recognize their employer as an insurer of their work, but they understand that their company provides them with security. They generally view their relationship with the owners of the firm as mutually beneficial. These workers' attempts to increase their productivity are consistent with the principle that reducing losses (such as wasted employee time) is beneficial to both insurer and insured.

Employees and employers should recognize their common interests, especially in a world of scarcity. In a period when the economic pie and the standard of living seem reluctant to grow, when people are disappointed with the purchasing power of their wages and salaries, and when the real value of savings is being diminished by inflation, the ire of employees exacerbates the traditional antagonisms between them and their employers. Yet such times call for more cooperation in the economy, for concerted efforts to increase the size of the economic pie.

The conclusion that capitalism is just is valid only when the system functions properly. Investors may do their jobs—insure work—but the role of investors is voluntary. Indeed, the unemployment problems in many countries indicate that investors do not always insure enough work. A system that prevents millions of people from working to support themselves is certainly not operating justly.

Much remains to be said about unemployment and other ailments that prevent capitalist systems from living up to their potential. But first we continue our evaluation of capitalism by looking at the record to see how effective this system has been at providing consumers—particularly those who are also workers—with goods and services.

# 9

# American Capitalism Is a Bargain

Which system provides more for its consumers—capitalism or socialism? Capitalism is frequently heralded as the champion. Yet under capitalism, some consumers receive economic pie with income from profits, not from wages or salaries. A more pointed version of the question is, therefore, Which system provides more for its *workers*? If we compare the best performances of each system, the answer is still capitalism. In the United States and other leading industrial countries, the proportion of the pie bought with profits is smaller than almost everybody imagines.

Claims about capitalism's productivity relative to socialism's are bandied about so much that examining actual data is worthwhile. Every year the World Bank compiles economic and other data about the countries of the world. For 1979, the latest year for which this information has been published, 124 countries were accounted for. One of the statistics the bank furnishes is per-capita gross national product (total output divided by population), which indicates how effective an economy is at turning out goods and services. But not all of these goods and services are produced for domestic consumers. So even if per-capita GNP is accurately measured, it is not a perfect index for comparing the standards of living of various countries. For example, in Israel a large part of gross national product is devoted to defense goods and services, leaving less for consumers. In Japan, on the other hand, where the military takes a relatively tiny portion of GNP, the consumers enjoy a larger share.

129

The World Bank warns us of the imperfections of these statistics. "Readers should exercise caution in comparing indicators across countries. . . . *The data should thus be construed only as indicating trends and characterizing major differences between countries*" (emphasis added).

The 20 countries with the highest per-capita GNP, and presumably the highest standards of living, are shown in the following table.

| Rank | Country | Per Capita GNP 1979 |
|------|---------|---------------------|
| 1 | Kuwait* | $17,100 |
| 2 | Switzerland | 13,920 |
| 3 | Sweden | 11,930 |
| 4 | Denmark | 11,900 |
| 5 | West Germany | 11,730 |
| 6 | Belgium | 10,920 |
| 7 | Norway | 10,700 |
| 8 | United States | 10,630 |
| 9 | Netherlands | 10,230 |
| 10 | France | 9,950 |
| 11 | Canada | 9,640 |
| 12 | Australia | 9,120 |
| 13 | Japan | 8,810 |
| 14 | Austria | 8,630 |
| 15 | Libya* | 8,170 |
| 16 | Finland | 8,160 |
| 17 | Saudi Arabia* | 7,280 |
| 18 | East Germany† | 6,430 |
| 19 | United Kingdom | 6,320 |
| 20 | New Zealand | 5,930 |

*capital-surplus oil exporters
†centrally planned economies
(Source: *World Development Report, 1981*, published for the World Bank by Oxford University Press.)

Kuwait, the first country on the list, as well as Saudi Arabia and Libya have small populations and huge exports of petroleum. Their economic systems have little to do with their large gross national products. A nation does not need a productive economic system in order to become rich by allowing foreign companies to tap its vast oil reserves. Of the remaining 17 countries on the list, all but one has a capitalist economy. The lone country in which the means of production are almost entirely owned and operated by the state is East Germany. You can find it near the bottom.

Some people may claim that Sweden, for example, which is renowned for its extensive welfare programs, and France, which has an avowedly socialist government, are socialist. Yet private investors own the preponderance of industrial and commercial enterprises. The Swedish government accounts for less than 10% of the production of manufacturers and for virtually none of the distribution of goods.

A capitalist country is one in which private enterprise accounts for most of the national product. *The most productive nations on earth, the ones that can be counted on to produce the largest per-capita GNP, are capitalist.*

Capitalism is realistic. Human beings usually put self-interest ahead of altruism. Capitalism takes constructive advantage of this facet of human nature; socialism makes believe that it does not exist. In a capitalist economy that works properly, the interests of individuals and society coincide. The system rewards investors in accordance with their contributions to production. Ironically, socialism, a system conceived by idealists, is less successful at linking individuals' self-interest to the general welfare.

Under capitalism, even an insensitive man who would not pause to help a blind person across the street develops an interest in other people's wants and whims when he contemplates investing in a business. He ponders whether families will be more eager to have computers in their kitchens, solar collectors on their roofs, or video recorders in their living rooms; whether business will benefit more from a company that delivers packages to distant destinations within 18 hours or from an information-retrieval system. The accuracy of the answers to these questions is important to him because his financial well-being depends on them.

Planners in a socialist economy may care a great deal about how various undertakings will satisfy the wants of the public—but they may not. Their self-interest requires that they protect their positions and their prestige by pleasing their superiors and staying out of trouble.

Capitalism entices people to take worthwhile risks by offering large rewards. It gives those who assume the risks of production a chance to increase their wealth considerably, and thus encourages

innovation in products and in production methods. Some of capitalism's most dramatic achievements occur when investors assume
large risks. Society took notable strides forward when investors
backed Cyrus McCormick, Thomas Edison, Henry Ford, and George
Eastman. The shareholders who were rewarded generously for risking their funds on such budding enterprises helped change the way
we live. Had these ventures failed, they would have sustained substantial losses.

Unlike capitalism, socialism does not encourage risk-taking. A
socialist official has little incentive to start a new enterprise or enlarge an existing one. If such a project is deemed unsuccessful, he
could lose his job. If it succeeds, his gain will be a commendation,
at best a promotion. Succeed or not, such a venture would cost him
time, energy, and sleep. He often prefers to leave things the way
they are.

Those capitalist societies that succeed in exploiting self-interest
will continue to bake bigger pies than socialist systems, which are,
at least theoretically, based on an idealistic view of human attitudes.
But the mere presence of a capitalist system does not guarantee that
consumers will have automobiles, TVs, automatic washing machines—or even enough to eat. Such countries as Bangladesh, In-
dia, and Ghana are low on the World Bank's list of productivity.
Each one's per-capita output is less than 1/25 of the United States'.

A dearth of resources, dense populations, and more than 50%
illiteracy contribute to the poverty of many countries, but these circumstances do not explain or excuse the poor showing of some capitalist economies. For example, the World Bank's list (see the following table) includes nations that are rich in resources, far from
overcrowded, and still have a much smaller per-capita gross national
product than the better-performing capitalist countries or even the
most productive socialist ones. The political, social, and cultural institutions in these countries prevent capitalism from attaining a high
degree of effectiveness. Because of price-fixing, officials' conflicts
of interest, fraud and deception, and other practices that interfere
with competition, a large proportion of these economies' profits go
to investors who do not earn them. Since these profits do not in-

duce any production or employment, they are wasted.

| Rank | Country | Per-Capita GNP 1979 |
|------|---------|--------------------:|
| 37 | Argentina | $2,230 |
| 43 | Brazil | 1,780 |
| 45 | Chile | 1,690 |
| 46 | Mexico | 1,640 |
| 77 | Bolivia | 550 |

In those capitalist economies where most of the profits go to investors who do earn them, the economic pie is not only larger than in socialist economies, it is also "tastier." Capitalism is sensitive to the varied tastes of consumers. Private business offers buyers wide choices and caters to their individual wants.

To survive in a competitive, capitalist market, an enterprise must be more responsive to consumer desires than it would have to be if it were part of a government-owned monopoly. A diligent socialist manager asks himself only if a product will be good enough to satisfy consumers. A capitalist businessman must endeavor to outdo competitors by continually striving to improve his company's products. "Good enough" may not be good enough. The result of the "natural selection" that occurs in markets is a superior choice of goods and services under capitalism.

Many thoughtful Americans have at one time or another wondered whether capitalism provides too wide a selection. Eight brands of tea and six of instant coffee on a supermarket shelf may seem wasteful. In the opinion of many individuals, the economy would be more efficient if it offered only one of each. Yet who would determine which one? "Experts" do tell us which wine we ought to drink with fettuccine Veronese and what we should wear when we talk to our banker about a loan. Even so, individuals in the more successful capitalist countries can choose their experts as well as the goods and services they want to buy.

What happens in a free market is a continuing election, one which makes certain that the candidates are responsive to the voters. A consumer may have a choice among, say, Zenith, RCA, Magnavox, and Sony. When he buys a Zenith, he is casting an extremely effective ballot for his favorite. The election determines which firms will provide which goods and services. Better examples of democracy in action are difficult to find.

If the consumer is a resident of the Soviet Union, he cedes the decision of what kind of TV he will buy to a bureaucracy. The authority of the state supersedes the preferences of the consumer. This system is a kind of economic tyranny.

Now we can conclude that a reasonably well-functioning capitalist system serves the average consumer by producing not only more goods and services but more desirable ones than even the best-run socialist economy. But we have not seen how well these two economic systems provide for the average *worker*. To do so, we must look at the portion of the economic pie that goes to investors in a capitalist country.

Across America, at country club after country club, the parking lots are showcases of wealth on wheels. On a languorous summer evening, any one of them may hold $2 million worth of motor vehicles. All those Mercedes-Benzes, Cadillacs, Lincolns, and the occasional Jaguars suggest that some people are consuming big pieces of the economic pie. Investors, of course! Or are they? Are those luxurious automobiles really purchased with profits?

Most of them are not. Most of them are driven either by well-paid employees of corporations or by the affluent self-employed: bankers, doctors, management consultants, financial experts, lawyers, marketing executives, star entertainers, and other high-status workers who derive incomes by performing productive tasks rather than by venturing their capital. Expensive automobiles are also provided for important employees of governments.

We are not criticizing the extra-large slices of pie consumed by prosperous workers. We are merely indicating that profits are not the sole source of purchasing power of the affluent. Even in socialist countries, some fortunate individuals enjoy large, indeed lavish, slices of the economic pie, although they receive no profits. In the Soviet Union, that bastion of Marxist equality, the standard of living of the upper-echelon officials, artists, scientists, and so forth does not appear to be exactly what the authors of *The Communist Manifesto* had in mind. Continentals and Cadillacs may not be much in evidence, but their places are filled by Zil and Chaika limousines.

Let's see how large a portion of the economic pie investors consume in the United States. We will look at the income received by investors, and compare it to total personal income. We want to emphasize again that, particularly in this country, investors are *not* a separate class from workers. Most middle- and upper-income individuals play more than one role—they are both investors and workers. Investors' income is the amount of money people receive from their investment activities whether they happen to be employees or not.

The income that investors receive can be divided into four categories. First, corporations pay them dividends, disbursements from profits.

Second, they receive interest from many sources. Interest is a kind of income different from profits, according to the Department of Commerce's national income statistics, CPAs' statements of corporate income, and the Internal Revenue Code. Still, because some economic theories consider interest to be the "profit on lending money," we will take notice of this kind of investor income.

Third, capitalist income includes capital gains—that is, gains on the sale of property. Even though investors refer to them as "profits," capital gains, as we explained earlier, have nothing to do with the flow of profits into the economy. Nevertheless, we will examine the effect of capital gains on the distribution of the economic pie.

Fourth, investors may receive profits from their noncorporate businesses. For example, a woman who finances her son's optometry shop, an unincorporated enterprise, receives a monetary return on her investment.

These four ways of acquiring purchasing power—dividends, interest, capital gains, and unincorporated-business profits—represent the investors' access to the economic pie. Of course, investors do not spend all of this income. When they forgo purchases of consumer goods and services—when they save—they are not taking any economic pie that would otherwise go to workers. People in high tax brackets usually save greater portions of their incomes than average working Americans. Thus, a dollar of after-tax income received by an affluent investor does not generally represent as much consumption as does a dollar of after-tax income paid to a teacher or assembly worker.

In 1979 (the latest year for which all data needed for the discussion in this chapter were available as these pages were being written), American corporations had after-tax profits of $168 billion, but most of these profits never reached investors. Some of this corporate income was used to finance purchases of capital and inventory goods. Some was needed for working capital to meet day-to-day expenses, which were rising as a result of expansion and inflation.

Corporations paid less than a third of their profits, $50 billion, to investors as dividends. These dividends were 2.6% of personal income, which totaled $1,944 billion. (The Department of Commerce defines "personal income" as the total current income of persons, the sum of all employee compensation, proprietors' income, dividends, personal interest income, rental income, and transfer payments—largely social security, pension, and welfare payments.) Let's see how much of the dividends went to affluent investors.

A significant portion of total dividends provides income for retirees by contributing to pension funds. In 1979, about 3% of total dividends, $1.5 billion, was paid to state and local government funds for policemen, garbage collectors, teachers, judges, governors, and so forth. Some of these public employees were already retired; others, who were still working, looked forward to enjoying their pensions in the future. Not many of these people fit the stereotype of the rich investor.

While state and local governments provide some especially generous pension plans, most of these programs are sponsored by private enterprises—some by unions. The private pension funds collected about 11% of the dividends paid in 1979. The profits that are paid into these institutions for the benefit of present and future retirees are hardly purchasing power for a capitalist class.

Any humane society supports its elderly and disabled members. No matter how these people obtain their purchasing power—from state benefit payments, personal savings, or privately administered pension funds—they consume a share of the economic pie. The standard of living of active workers is affected by how much of the pie nonworking consumers obtain, but not by how these people acquire the money they spend. Thus, most dividends that help to support retired workers are not a cost of capitalism—retirees and those unable to work should have some of the available goods and services under any system.

If pensions are socially valuable forms of income, so are the dividends paid to educational institutions and foundations. These organizations received about 4% of total dividends in 1978. Additional dividends went to various other nonprofit institutions.

About 80% of dividends did not become pension benefits or support nonprofit organizations but were paid to individual investors. These funds were only 2% of personal income ("persons" as defined by the Department of Commerce includes pension funds and nonprofit institutions as well as individuals), and since the recipients of these dividends were generally in higher tax brackets than the rest of the population, this income was taxed more heavily than the average wage or salary income. As a result, less than 2% of disposable (after-tax) personal income came from the dividends paid to individuals in 1979.

Whether interest, the second source of investor income, is profits or not has long been debated, and we doubt that the issue will be resolved soon. Even if the interest on a bond issued by the American Telephone and Telegraph Company is deemed to be profits, what is the interest on a U.S. government savings bond? Or the interest on a deposit at the neighborhood savings and loan association? Regardless of whether interest is profits or not, it is investor's income.

The total monetary interest in 1979, $139 billion, was 7% of personal income. Two-thirds of this interest came from savings deposits at banks and similar institutions. Whether or not the recipients of this income were investors earning profits, they were in most cases middle-income Americans who are not popularly thought of as being either capitalists or wealthy.

The interest received by pension funds for the benefit of employees certainly did not increase the purchasing power of investors at the expense of workers. As in the case of dividends, a small part of total interest went to pension funds and to educational and other nonprofit institutions.

Affluent people who received interest income probably got most of it from treasury obligations, tax-free state and local bonds, corporate paper, or mortgages. Interest from these sources totaled less than 2½% of personal income in 1979.

Americans who received interest income in 1979 actually suffered a loss. In order to receive $139 billion in interest, persons had savings of $1.7 trillion in credit-market instruments—bonds, mortgages, and so forth—and in time and savings deposits. But because of inflation, the purchasing power of these savings depreciated about 13%, or $230 billion. Even before taxes, owners of the $1.7-trillion savings had a real loss of $91 billion ($230–$139 billion). After taxes, they fared much worse. This was no way for capitalists to get rich.

(Our discussion of interest income has ignored "imputed interest," which is counted by the Department of Commerce as a part of personal income. This item is not monetary interest but the Department's valuation of the services rendered by banks, insurance companies, and other financial institutions to consumers by maintaining their accounts. Neither we nor the Internal Revenue Service consider imputed interest to be income.)

Great fortunes are not built with interest and dividends. Even if inflation were nonexistent, accumulating enough interest and dividend income to become rich would take more than one lifetime.

Capital gains are the stuff that makes people very rich. They are taxed at lower rates than wage, salary, dividend, and interest income. And best of all, they can sometimes be enormous. (Of course, so can capital losses.)

Capital gains are not profits—they have nothing to do with the economy's flow of profits. They are, in a nutshell, the gain an investor enjoys when he sells an investment for more than he paid for it. A capital gain is realized, for example, when an individual who bought a portrait from a starving painter for $25 three years ago learns that the artist has been "discovered" and sells the work for $10,000. Another capital gain is realized when an entrepreneur who invested $100,000 in his business sells it for $2 million. Capital gains can come from sales of securities, antiques, real estate, copyrights, and so forth.

Yet capital gains do not give investors one cent of net purchasing power! A capital gain can only occur when one investor sells property to another investor. They merely exchange property. One gives the other money and gets a work of art, securities, or other assets. *The net holdings of the "investor class" are unchanged!*

Suppose a plumber who has saved for a number of years decides to buy a diamond from a friend, giving the latter a capital gain. The plumber is thereby transferring some of his purchasing power to his companion, yet this transaction is not a transfer of purchasing power from the "working class" to the "capitalist class." The worker who willingly trades away his current purchasing power and gets the chance of enjoying future capital gains himself makes the exchange as an investor. The rest of the workers in the country do not suffer because of his decision. They are unaffected.

Even if capital gains did represent net income to all investors, and therefore a way for them to collectively increase their consumption at the expense of workers, the bite out of the pie would be small. In 1979, net realized capital gains amounted to about $54 billion, an amount less than 3% of the nation's total personal income. A large part of these capital gains resulted from the sales of homes by individuals, and virtually all of these gains reflected inflation. Capital gains had little if any effect on the standard of living of the working class.

The fourth source of investor income is noncorporate profits, which include both proprietors' and rental income. Rental income was $30.5 billion in 1979 according to the Department of Commerce. However, the Department included in its calculation nearly $12 billion of "rental income on owner occupied houses." (You read it right—the rent that people pay themselves for living in their own houses.) Rather than try to explain this peculiar statistic, let us simply note that it is a bookkeeping adjustment necessary to keep the national accounting straight, but not an actual source of income to anyone.

That leaves less than $19 billion of rental income—less than 1% of personal income. Some of this rent is collected by families that rent space in their houses, farmers who rent excess cropland, and other persons who rent some of their property for a few extra dollars. Few automobiles at country-club parking lots were purchased with personal rental income.

Proprietors' income is earned by farmers, shop owners, self-employed repairmen, and independent professionals—doctors, lawyers, accountants, and so forth. The income of (unincorporated) proprietors is their compensation for working: wages plus their profits as entrepreneurs. No one knows how much of this income is wages and how much is profits. Let us consider the case of a not atypical proprietor of a retail store who works long hours six days a week. If he had to pay one or more employees to do his work—ordering new inventory, selling, keeping books, and so forth—his payroll might well exceed his present income. Thus, little of the proprietors' income should be regarded as profits.

Proprietors' income in 1979 was $117 billion, close to 7% of personal income. That even $10 billion of this amount was profits is unlikely.

During our examination of the four kinds of investment income, we said little about the presence of an extremely wealthy class. But a considerable number of people in this country *are* very rich. They own the yachts moored along Florida's inland waterway, mansions atop mountains, and paintings by Impressionist masters. They buy wine at auctions for thousands of dollars a bottle, travel to exotic places in grand style, and throw extravagant parties. Who are these people?

They are individuals who enjoy the purchasing power obtained from enormous capital gains. Some of them are innovative industrialists or shrewd merchant princes. Some of them are investors who astutely (or luckily) chose to back corporations that later became storybook successes. And some of these multimillionaires are the heirs of such fortune builders.

But not all conspicuous consumption is attributable to investors spending their money. A piece of the economic pie goes to powerful individuals in the guise of business or government operating expenses. Top executives of corporations fly in company jets to conduct business on golf courses in faraway places. Some state governors and mayors of major cities are provided with mansions staffed with public employees. Many elite members of both the business and government sectors are chauffeured about in limousines paid for by corporations or taxpayers.

Furthermore, because labor markets for top managers do not always work well, or even adequately, some presidents and other executive officers are able to determine their own salaries, stock options, and pensions. These upper-echelon employees help to set high standards for the remuneration of the heads of other corporations. Investors are not the only ones to receive copious slices of the economic pie.

Nor are investors and their representatives, top management, the only people who use their power to acquire far above average quantities of goods and services. This phenomenon is not confined to capitalists, or even to capitalist nations. Some union leaders seem to have standards of living as high as the heads of the corporations with whom they bargain over wages and working conditions. High officials in the Soviet Union live lavishly. The people who make important decisions about the allocation of resources, wherever they may be, have predilections toward allocating generous portions to themselves. They often consume king-size slices of the pie—at the expense of other consumers.

We do not count the corporate jets, the executive retreats on tropical islands, or company limousines as a cost of American capitalism. Such amenities are not purchased by individuals with their shares of the economy's profits. They are the trappings of power, the access to goods and services that tends to appear in all countries no matter who owns the means of production.

Elite workers are not the only ones who consume more than Department of Commerce statistics would lead us to believe. Many workers below the top ranks of management collect extra pieces of the pie by padding their expense accounts or by legitimately consuming goods and services at company expense. Sales representatives, engineers, accountants, technicians, and others travel on business. Often their companies reimburse them not only for fares and lodging but for drinks, entertainment, and deluxe accommodations.

Moreover, rather than purchase a sandwich and a cup of coffee at the corner delicatessen, businessmen frequently enjoy "three-martini lunches" with clients or associates—on the company.

Many workers also earn significant amounts of money that are not included in the personal-income statistics by working in the "underground economy." An auto-repair business hires a part-time mechanic and pays him cash while entering some other expense in the books. A carpenter converts a neighbor's porch into a room without reporting the income to the Internal Revenue Service.

Data on the volume of unreported transactions in the United States is of course unavailable, but estimates of the amount run into hundreds of billions of dollars. Moonlighters are especially tempted to join the underground economy because the income from their second jobs raises their tax bracket. Besides, supplementary income is often easy to hide. Retired people may join the underground economy in order to receive additional income without losing some of their social security payments.

To the extent that workers' income is larger than we previously assumed, our estimates of the proportion of the economic pie consumed by investors diminishes.

People could argue forever about precisely how to define "investor income." Moreover, no statistics exist that can tell us exactly how much of this income is used to purchase economic pie at workers' expense. Nevertheless, the available data help to put the size of investor income in perspective. We conclude that investor income was about 2%—at most 3%—of personal income in 1979. We count only the dividends that went to individuals, and small parts of rental and proprietors' income. Investments in interest-bearing obligations sustained losses after allowing for inflation. And capital gains do not represent a change in the wealth of the investing class.

Of course, the aggregate value of the corporations that investors own does increase over a period of time. Indeed, in an expanding economy, this increase is prodigious. But the ownership of wealth is not the same as consumption of the economic pie, a distinction dramatized by the story of a man whose grandfather bequeathed 500 shares of stock to him in 1950 with the stern advice, "Never sell

IBM." The heir lived modestly, watched the value of his shares multiply, and had trouble paying his monthly bills. Of course, most affluent people indulge themselves more than this owner of IBM. Still, much personal wealth tends to accumulate without being converted into consumption. Indeed, if all the investors in the country ever tried to cash in their investments at once and go on spending sprees, the market values of their holdings would collapse. We have difficulty imagining any circumstances under which investor wealth would seriously impinge on the American worker's share of the pie. Therefore, workers concerned about their portion of the economic pie need worry only about the size of the slice investors consume and not about the value of the investors' portfolios.

However one chooses to calculate investor income, American capitalism is a bargain for the "working class." Even an exaggerated tabulation of profits—one that included capital gains, interest income before taxes and inflation, and dividends paid to pension funds as capitalist income—would not yield a figure much over 12% of personal income. Meanwhile, Americans have capitalism to thank for producing one of the world's highest standards of living. The U.S. per-capita gross national product is almost twice that of the most successful socialist country.

Although the cost of capitalism in the United States in recent times has been small, we cannot conclude that capitalism is a bargain everywhere at all times. When we look at some capitalist countries, where masses are fortunate to have enough to eat while a few investors live in splendor, we cannot help believing that inordinately large shares of the meager economic pies are going to these capitalists. Competition is not doing its job. Profits are being wasted.

Here and in chapter 8, we have seen that capitalism can be both just and productive. However, no economy lives up to its potential when large numbers of workers cannot find employment. When a willing and able worker cannot find a job, the economy is not just. When a significant portion of society's human resources is not used, the economy is not fully productive. We therefore turn our attention to the problem of unemployment in a capitalist economy.

# 10

# Profits and Employment

As we know all too well, even the advanced capitalist economies sometimes stumble. For months or years at a time, their economies fail to work properly, and unemployment becomes a problem. The consequences may be disastrous, as they were during the Great Depression, or moderately disturbing, as in the mild 1960–61 American recession. During the 1970s, unemployment in the United States was chronic. It became increasingly serious as the decade progressed. As we entered the 1980s, America was experiencing lingering unemployment, an undesirable situation that had not substantially improved for a full decade.

What causes these periods of economic malaise? Why does a nation like the United States sometimes enjoy a period of phenomenal prosperity and progress and then a spell when its economy does not make full use of the work force? Workers are no less eager for employment than at any other time, and investors are as hungry for profits as ever. Markets have not lost their ability to allocate resources, nor have the statutes, regulations, and customs that help control economies changed significantly.

The trouble is that investors are not insuring enough work. Because their role is voluntary, they will not play it unless they think that their self-interest will be served—unless they believe that the prospects of profit justify their assuming the risks of production and marketing.

Were capitalism not able to give men and women the fundamental right to work productively in order to support themselves, the system would have a serious, inherent deficiency. But unemployment is *not* an inevitable development in a capitalist economy. Unemployment is a result of neglect or mismanagement of the system. It can be avoided if the economy generates sufficient profits and if they are distributed equitably—that is, if they go to those who *earn* them.

In this world, with an endless list of tasks to be performed, any economic arrangements that prevent eager men and women from putting their energies and talents to work are ironic and intolerable. The failure to achieve full employment is a tragedy not only for individuals unable to find work but also for societies that suffer widespread joblessness.

"Full employment" does not mean that every member of the labor force currently has a job. It occurs when every person who is willing and able to work can find a job. Even with "full employment," three kinds of unemployment exist.

The first of these is not a problem. A healthy capitalist economy always has some people who are temporarily without jobs but who can readily find new, satisfactory ones. Some of these unemployed workers have voluntarily left positions in order to move to other parts of the country, change careers, find more congenial employers, and so forth. Others have been dismissed from firms that were unable to meet competition and therefore had to curtail their operations. In some cases, employees have been discharged merely because their bosses personally disliked them. Whatever the reason for their joblessness, as long as these workers can readily find suitable new employment, their transitional state of idleness is no cause for concern.

More painful is the predicament of a worker who becomes "technologically unemployed"—the victim of modernization, labor-saving machines, or new processes. If the economy is working properly, it will generate enough jobs so that these individuals will be able to find employment. However, they may no longer be able to use their specialized skills; they may have to take lower-status, lower-paying, and less interesting jobs. The frequent claim that technological progress increases unemployment is incorrect, but it can create difficulties for individuals.

When an industry loses some jobs to labor-saving innovations, employment opportunities tend to appear in other industries. A good example is farming. In 1900, nearly 11 million people—40% of the labor force—were employed on American farms. Today there are less than 3½ million, well under 4% of all workers. The development of machinery, hybrid crops, new breeding techniques, chemical fertilizers, and so forth have made farmers vastly more productive than they were 80 years ago. The loss of nearly 8 million farm jobs during this period did not cause a huge increase in unemployment. Other industries absorbed the displaced workers.

If technological progress caused capitalism to malfunction, America would be wise to shop for a new system. Fortunately, capitalism thrives on progress. Those who advocate restraining the application of technology in order to prevent greater unemployment do not understand the system. As we will see shortly, national employment has risen and fallen over the years in response to one crucial phenomenon: changes in the flow of profits.

The third kind of unemployment that exists during "full employment" is a serious problem. Unfortunately, many of the people who are unemployed today are willing but, for all practical purposes, *unable* to contribute to production. These individuals are unskilled, and some of them may be illiterate, inexperienced, or unable to speak English. A few of them do not even understand the importance of showing up on time, following directions, or interacting civilly with fellow employees.

At present, compared to 50 years ago, only a small proportion of the nation's jobs can be performed by illiterate, unskilled people, even if they are diligent. Only a limited number of positions exist for dishwashers, floor sweepers, and so forth. Even when the want ads are filled with openings for secretaries, electricians, and salespersons, opportunities will be scarce for the man or woman who can hardly communicate with supervisors, customers, and other workers—let alone type, wire a circuit-breaker panel, or present a product to a potential buyer.

Ineffective schools, broken homes, discrimination, an erosion of the moral fiber of society, and combinations of these maladies are often blamed for rendering millions of people unemployable. Ironically, these social ills have been able to thrive largely because of the economy's repeated failures to provide enough jobs. When economic conditions force productive workers into chronic unemployment, they and their children are likely to fall victims to poverty and demoralization. The chances of the children learning to be constructive members of the labor force diminish. Thus, unemployment can lead to unemployability.

We hesitate to assert that anyone is unfit to work. Undoubtedly some individuals have severe physical, mental, or psychological handicaps. There are also some unemployed people whose willingness to work is dubious. Nevertheless, many so-called unemployables can be trained to be productive workers if enough time and effort are invested in them.

Given the right economic conditions, business will make substantial efforts to train workers. When the economy is moving along at a healthy pace and firms are eager to hire additional personnel, individuals with few qualifications begin to find opportunities. If employers have difficulty finding experienced workers, they will bear the costs of teaching new employees needed skills. Corporate training programs (including work-orientation courses that teach things as fundamental as discipline, persistence, and how to relate to employers and fellow workers) have been successful at transforming unskilled labor into productive employees.

On the other hand, when an economy is running at less than full capacity and large numbers of workers are idle, companies tend to employ those individuals who are already trained and experienced. New entrants to the labor force remain unemployed, and society begins to accumulate inexperienced, unskilled workers.

If the economy can provide a sufficient demand for workers, not only will those able and willing to work be able to find employment, but many of the unemployable will be transformed into able workers, and also hired. Successful economic policies may not obliterate crime, illiteracy, racism, and poverty, but they can create an environment in which these cruel social conditions may recede.

The key to solving the unemployment problem is profits. Give business sufficient incentive to expand its operations and it will create the jobs needed to achieve full employment. Individual industries expand and contract in response to changes in the amount of profits available. If enough of them enjoy increases in profitability, the business sector will raise production, accelerate investments in new facilities, and employ additional workers. If the flow of profits into the economy is adequate, it will lead to full employment.

(We emphasize that this discussion does not necessarily apply to economies where competition is seriously impeded. Markets must assure that profits go to firms that earn them—profits must not be wasted. Profits cannot cure unemployment in fundamentally corrupt economies where they do not motivate companies to expand.)

Changes in the flow of profits are responsible for the major variations in employment that occur over the course of a business cycle. Suppose the economy has been enjoying a high employment rate and then the flow of profits decreases. There are no longer enough profits in the economy for business to maintain both the profit margins and volume of sales that it has been experiencing. Competition becomes excessive in industries throughout the economy, firms discover that they cannot sell all the goods they expected to sell at the prices they expected to receive. Most of them respond to this situation by reducing prices in an effort to sell their products. Narrowing margins induce industries to shrink. Companies curtail production, cancel investment plans, and lay off workers. Some of them go out of business.

While many enterprises are dismissing employees, only a small number of firms are expanding their operations and hiring. Most laid-off workers have nowhere to go for new jobs. Thus, the decrease in the nation's aggregate profits leads to a decline in employment.

A small flow of profits can support only a small volume of business. As long as profits remain low, no recovery will begin. Without sufficient profits, the economy's potential production and full employment cannot be attained.

But suppose the flow from the profit sources strengthens. Firms in a wide variety of industries experience a strong increase in demand. They find that they can raise prices and still enjoy improved sales. As excessive competition abates, their profit margins, which had been suboptimum, become attractive. In order to take advantage of growing sales opportunities, companies increase production. They find that they need to rehire many of the workers they had laid off. Their capacity utilization rises, inducing executives to increase investment in new plant and equipment, creating additional jobs. If the flow of profits is strong enough, the widespread expansion will cause full employment.

Ideally, just enough profit should flow to business to assure that every available worker who can contribute to production has the opportunity for employment. But what if more profits flow into the business sector than this minimum amount? Firms in many industries will have inordinately high margins. Such margins are incentives to expand. Expansion would require additional employees, but business cannot hire more workers when no one is unemployed. Since the extra-wide margins serve no social purpose, they are excessive.

Excessive profit margins cause two problems. First, competition relaxes. Companies can afford to be less efficient and less responsive to consumer needs than formerly. Consequently, human and material resources are not used to the best advantage. Second, excessive margins mean excessive prices. Widening margins are one of the phenomena that can contribute to inflation.

Increases in the economy's flow of profits generally precede gains in employment. There are several reasons for the delayed effect. First, most companies are not sure that their profits are rising until they have experienced improved business for several weeks. Second, more time usually passes before executives decide to expand production and hire additional employees. Third, even after these decisions are made, the needed personnel must be recruited and selected. Fourth, a company must sometimes wait until it has received new materials or equipment—or constructed new plants—before it can use additional workers.

Decreases in profits, like increases, have a delayed effect on employment. Even when orders, sales, and profits are declining, firms are generally reluctant to discharge personnel. Most executives find that discharging employees is the most unpleasant task they encounter. In addition, if management believes that the company will need its currently superfluous personnel in the not too distant future, the cost of keeping them may be smaller than that of subsequently finding new workers and integrating them into the organization. Moreover, laying off employees lowers the morale of those who remain, increases the firm's unemployment-insurance taxes, and may oblige it to incur large severance-pay expenses. Only when the decline in profits is considerable and appears to be continuing do most companies begin to lay off personnel.

Since individual firms generally need time to increase or decrease the number of workers they employ, one would expect the national statistics to show aggregate profits rising somewhat ahead of total employment. Indeed, the trend of employment does tend to lag behind the trend of profits.

Profits, then, are a portent of changes in general business conditions, in production, employment, and sales. Studies of the business cycle by the National Bureau of Economic Research have reached the conclusion that profitability is an early sign of what is to come, or, in terminology the NBER popularized, "a leading indicator."

If the government wants to keep the economy healthy, it must be sensitive to changes in the profit sources. It must also take steps to *affect* profits, to keep them flowing at an optimum rate. It must *manage* profits.

Yet when was the last time you heard a president of the United States tell the nation that to counter unemployment and recession, "business needs more profits"? When have you heard any public official, even a close friend of industry, discuss the condition of the economy in terms of the total amount of profits that is being secured and the amount that ought to be available to business?

The government's best tool for regulating the flow of profits is fiscal policy—the adjustment of its taxes and spending in order to produce a desired deficit or surplus. Government deficit is, of course, a source of profits, so fiscal policy is a direct way to adjust the flow of profits.

Deficit spending is a subject of controversy. Many economists and politicians have denounced it as inherently unsound, inflationary, and destructive. True, irresponsible government borrowing can have undesirable consequences. However, we will see in the next chapter that rising government debt, like expanding corporate debt, can contribute to business's ability to create a larger economic pie. The federal government can responsibly run deficits that strengthen rather than weaken the economy.

Governments have long known that rising deficits (or declining surpluses) "stimulate" the economy and, conversely, that diminishing deficits tend to slow it down. But they have not recognized the effect of these measures on profits.

Economists generally rely on John Maynard Keynes's explanation when confronting the issue of how a $1-billion increase in the government deficit results in several billion dollars of additional production. Keynes offered a mathematical description of this phenomenon, which does not describe many important aspects of the process. The Keynesian explanation centers on the effect of fiscal policy on national income, overlooking the crucial, initial effect on profits. Although Keynes did not discuss the role of profits in this process, his theory depends on firms responding to changes in their profits in the ways that we have described.

Partly because the effect of deficit spending on profits has not been understood, fiscal efforts to achieve prosperity have sometimes been excessive, other times inadequate. Moreover, a mythology about the effects of government deficits on inflation has sprouted.

As we have seen, the stimulus to the economy resulting from an increase in the government deficit is really an increase in profits. As firms struggle to win the new profits, competitive forces induce them to expand their operations and increase employment. By focusing on the profit sources, the government can see more clearly what it is doing to the economy as it adjusts its fiscal activities. The federal government may determine that profits of less than, for example, $200 billion will lead to unemployment, and that profits of more than $220 billion will be excessive. Once the target is set, government should adopt the tax changes or other measures needed to keep the flow of profits in the desirable range.

For government to successfully manage the flow of profits, the confusion that has dominated national debates about federal budgets must be dispelled. If the majority of elected officials understood and shared the goal of optimizing the flow of profits, formulating fiscal policy would become a more rational process. But as long as some segments of the public and their representatives seek a balanced budget as an ultimate economic goal while others insist on cutting taxes, and the rest hold conflicting views, politics will continue to complicate and obfuscate the issue.

Once officials understood how an optimum surplus or deficit contributes to stability and full employment, they could take steps to attain this fiscal goal. Government's first task in managing profits would be keeping them and their sources under careful surveillance. Forecasting the trend of profits should be part of this operation. Despite profits' volatility, their trend can be predicted with sufficient accuracy once their sources are understood. (We make this assertion with confidence because one of us has been forecasting profits for 40 years.) Even a reasonably accurate appraisal of current profits will give the government time to adopt measures that will prevent the flow of profits from becoming either excessive or insufficient—time to prevent any marked and sustained decrease in employment or competition.

Second, government should determine what budget deficit or surplus is necessary at any time in order to keep profits flowing into the economy at an optimum rate. When it prepares its annual budget, it should consider the optimum deficit or surplus to be an imperative and determine spending and taxation policies accordingly.

Third, government should have the flexibility to change personal income tax rates every six months in case adjustments to the surplus or deficit become necessary. Then it could make the timely decisions that will maintain stable prosperity.

There are other ways, less desirable than fiscal policy adjustments, to regulate the flow of profits. The government—or more precisely its central bank, the Federal Reserve—can affect the flow of profits indirectly by influencing investment and consumption decisions. The Federal Reserve can more or less determine how much credit banks can extend or how high or low interest rates will be. As credit becomes more readily available and interest rates more attractive, businesses and consumers tend to incur more debt. Business borrowing usually increases investments in new fixed assets or inventories—both of which are sources of profits. Consumer borrowing represents a reduction in personal saving—a negative source of profits. Thus, both business and consumer borrowing contribute to the flow of profits.

But the Federal Reserve should not design monetary policy to influence the flow of profits. For reasons we will discuss in the next chapter, attempts to use monetary policy to combat inflation seriously impair the ability of markets to serve society.

The government can try to influence the other profit sources besides its own surplus or deficit, but in so doing it is unlikely to significantly or quickly affect the flow of profits. It is likely to produce harmful side effects. Government might, for example, try to influence the nation's volume of exports and imports in order to increase or reduce net foreign investment. The effect on this source of profits would at most be small. Unfortunately, the adverse consequences for domestic consumers, U.S. relations with other countries, and the efficiency of American industry could be serious.

Washington might also try to encourage business to increase or decrease inventories or pay more or less dividends. Such actions would do more harm than good. Markets rather than government should influence these decisions.

Another way for the government to influence the flow of profits is through policies that encourage fixed investment, a major profit source. For example, the Japanese government has received considerable attention because of the way it supports fledgling industries with strategic economic importance or growth potential. And in the United States, the government has for decades used tax incentives to encourage businesses in general to invest in capital goods. It has also taken measures to foster investment in housing by subsidizing some construction projects and guaranteeing millions of mortgages.

Although these government programs may affect investment, we do not recommend them as tools for regulating the flow of profits. Since such policies influence profits only indirectly, they are less precise than fiscal policies. Even more important, these measures may have harmful side effects. They should be evaluated on their costs and benefits aside from their influence on the flow of profits.

Unemployment is a gauge of failure. If the system does not provide a job for everyone who is willing and able to contribute to the production of goods and services, it fails both individuals and society. Because government can readily avoid such a failure, it is ultimately to blame for unemployment.

Many politicians and economists realize that there are means to create jobs, but they hesitate to use them for fear that they will exacerbate inflation. Because inflation is widely misunderstood, our officials have been unable to find constructive ways to contend with rising prices. Out of desperation, they have resorted to misguided fiscal and monetary policies that have resulted in chronic unemployment. An understanding of inflation is therefore necessary not only to control upward pressures on prices but also to end government-sponsored unemployment. Since prices are monetary phenomena, we turn our attention to money.

# 11

# Money, Credit, and Profits

The pages of theory and empirical observations on money and the banking system stretch from here to the top of the national debt. But this massive accumulation of knowledge, like the work of scholars in other areas of economics, is sorely lacking in one respect: little attention is paid to profits.

We use a common definition of "money": a medium of exchange, a means of payment. This definition describes the money flowing between sectors of our "pipeline economy." Thus, currency, checks, and charge-card and other forms of credit are money. (Of course, "money" has many other useful definitions, including the formulas that are regularly mentioned in the financial press, M1 and M2.)

Our discussion of the role of money has important implications for both monetary and fiscal policy. Government's role in promoting full employment and stable prices becomes clearer as we examine money and credit, and how they affect profits.

Profits are the lifeblood of business, and credit is the lifeblood of profits. Five of the sources of profits are directly nourished by credit: fixed investment, changes in inventories, negative personal saving, net foreign investment, and government deficit. These profit sources are *credit-sensitive*— each of them depends on borrowing. (Dividends and profits taxes, which are not on the foregoing list, represent the recirculation of profits already secured and are thus only indirectly affected by credit. Capital consumption allowances

155

largely reflect past purchases of capital goods and have nothing to do with the current use of money or credit.)

Usually the biggest source of profits is *fixed investment*. Without credit, most of the nation's investment in capital goods would cease and profits would be drastically reduced. Builders finance nearly all structures almost entirely with credit. Were it not for building and mortgage loans, virtually no one would invest in a shopping center or an apartment house. A large proportion of equipment is purchased with money borrowed from banks, other financial institutions, or individual bondholders. Railroad cars, commercial airliners, and cargo ships often bear inscribed brass plates certifying that some financial institutions have liens on the conveyances as a result of having loaned the money to buy them.

*Changes in inventories* are also highly dependent on the use of credit. Farmers rely on bank loans to finance their crops until they are sold. Stores borrow in order to increase their inventories for the Christmas shopping season. In any season, producers and distributors who borrow to carry inventories are major customers of most banks.

*Personal saving* is a negative source of profits. ("Personal saving" is the name used to describe the net amount of consumer saving and consumer borrowing, as illustrated in Fig. 10, p. 64.) When consumers borrow, personal saving declines, and profits increase.

*Net foreign investment* usually makes a slight positive contribution to the flow of American profits. Because both exports and imports are often financed by credit, a total absence of borrowed funds would have only a small net effect on this profit source. But in order to be able to export to less-developed countries, the United States has to lend them especially large sums. Without credit, our net foreign investment would therefore decrease.

The last credit-sensitive source of profits is the *government deficit*. Federal, state, and local governments finance outlays that exceed their receipts with either borrowed money or previously accumulated cash. Since most of them, including the federal government, seldom have any savings, practically all deficits are totally financed by debt.

The total profits of the business sector in 1980 were $245 billion.

Without the credit-sensitive profit sources, which totaled $378 billion, the business sector would have lost $133 billion. *Credit is not only important to the health of our capitalist system; it is essential for its existence.* When the government considers any policy or action that would affect lending on a national scale, it ought to take into account the economy's sensitivity to major changes in the extension of credit.

Money is created by banks when they extend credit. For example, a bank lends $500,000 to a lawn-mower manufacturer to finance its production for the coming season. The banker does not hand over a stack of five hundred $1,000 bills but instead writes "$500,000" in the credit column of the company's checking account. Some of this money, usually a small fraction of the total, is the bank's own funds, its reserves. The rest, most of the $500,000, is new money coming into the world—by the stroke of a pen.

The manufacturer writes checks all during the winter to pay for the labor, materials, rent, and other expenses involved in the assembly of mowers. As his bank balance is gradually reduced, the bank-account balances of his employees and suppliers rise as they deposit the checks. They in turn purchase goods and services with the money that was created out of thin air by a bank.

When borrowers repay their bank loans, money is taken out of circulation. Eventually the manufacturer sells his lawn mowers. He then has enough money in his account to repay the loan. When he is ready to do so, the bank takes $500,000 out of his checking account. Money vanishes by another stroke of the pen.

Is inflation caused by banks creating too much money? "Yes," says popular erudition. "Too many dollars are chasing too few goods. The banks should not create so much money. They must not be allowed to write so many loans."

How many dollars should "chase" goods? That is, how much money should flow into the business sector as payment for its products? The answer: enough to equal the business sector's expense plus optimum profits—the minimum amount of profits that will induce business to create enough jobs for full employment. As long as business can sell virtually everything it produces and collect optimum profits, the right amount of dollars will be "chasing" goods.

Inflation or no inflation, if business *cannot* sell the goods and services it produces at prices that provide acceptable profits, the system will stumble. Profits, production, and employment will fall—in that order. So, to keep the economy from faltering, enough money must flow into the business sector.

The fear of "too many dollars" is based on the idea that they will be used to bid prices up to excessive levels. Of course, such excessive prices would mean that businesses were enjoying unnecessarily wide profit margins. But as long as businesses are earning optimum profit margins, they are not charging excessive prices. They are charging the prices they need to cover their expenses and risks. *Excessive growth of the money supply cannot create "excessive demand" and thus bid prices up unless it widens profit margins.* If the nation's flow of profits remains optimum or less, "too many dollars" cannot be blamed for fueling inflation. Instead, rising business costs must be the culprit.

Many people will disagree with this assertion, insisting that if the amount of money in the system were limited, prices could not rise, and neither could costs. But, as we will see, the United States is in an era in which powerful long-term forces having little or nothing to do with the amount of money in the economy are pushing business costs higher. Rising labor costs are not caused by readily available credit, and in fact are largely unaffected by the supply of money unless that amount is so inadequate that the economy is seriously damaged. Other costs, such as the real prices of imported materials, would be rising because of growing worldwide demand whether more dollars were chasing goods or not.

Profit margins are not always optimum, at least not if the economy is left entirely to its own devices. Although the system usually tends to generate the right amount of profits, it often produces a flow that is either inadequate or excessive. Under some conditions, the economy may fail to generate an optimum amount of profits for several consecutive years.

Thus the flow of profits must be managed, and our government in Washington has the power to do the job. Sometimes it should run a surplus, and sometimes a deficit. Yet government deficit spending is often called "unsound," "reckless," "irresponsible," and, above all, "inflationary"! Is it? Deficit spending deserves those epithets if it causes profit margins to rise beyond optimal levels. Excessive profits are always reflected in prices. But if deficit spending is used to maintain optimum profits, it will not contribute to a rise in prices. A government deficit that preserves optimum margins hardly affects the prices business pay for labor and imported materials. Since it contributes neither to excessive margins nor rising costs, it has no inflationary effect.

*Therefore, any federal deficit that maintains an optimum flow of profits to the business sector cannot cause inflation!* The popular notion of the early 1980s that deficit spending is inherently inflationary is a myth!

What about the claims that federal-government borrowing is unsound? Our national debt grows every year a deficit is incurred. In 1981, it was about a trillion dollars. Can we ever pay it back? Can we sleep knowing that this tremendous burden will hang over our children's heads?

Many of the people who share this concern are much less anxious about the debts of the business and household sectors. America's nonfinancial business owed about $1½ trillion in 1981. The debt of the household sector was about $1¼ trillion. In a capitalist economy, which depends on credit to create profits, how could debt be avoided?

Nevertheless, federal-government borrowing has some unique characteristics that may be disturbing. Washington has access to credit that is available to no other borrowers. When the Federal Reserve lends to the U.S. Treasury, it creates money—by the stroke of a pen—just as commercial banks do. However, when the federal government borrows from itself in this fashion, it does not have to answer the hard-nosed questions that lenders usually address to prospective borrowers to determine whether they are credit-worthy.

Yet when the federal government incurs consecutive deficits in order to maintain an optimum flow of profits, the resulting increase in the national debt is sound. Whenever Washington borrows—or saves—to control the flow of profits and keep the system running smoothly and efficiently, it is acting responsibly.

Although total debt—consumer, business, foreign, and government—must rise in a prosperous capitalist economy, the government debt in particular need not grow indefinitely. *If the business sector were using enough credit to purchase capital goods, the government would not have to make up for a shortfall in the flow of profits by increasing its own debt. Indeed, private investment would generally be sufficient were it not for monetary policies that discourage capital outlays.* Although the government would sometimes have to borrow, it would just as often have to save. Over a period of five or ten years, there would be little change in the government's overall financial position.

When the U.S. government does incur a deficit, its alleged profligacy is magnified by peculiarities in its accounting practices. The funds borrowed by the Treasury are not linked to particular expenditures; chance, not the government, determines which outlays use tax revenues and which use borrowed funds. All anyone knows is that deficit spending is needed because taxes are insufficient to meet outlays. No one can be sure whether a State Department banquet, a new submarine, a housing subsidy, or an appendectomy for a Medicaid patient is paid for with borrowed money. Among all the organizations in the economy—businesses, governments, and not-for-profit institutions, this lack of accounting precision is unique to Washington.

When a state or local jurisdiction borrows, the proceeds from its sale of bonds are generally earmarked for the acquisition of long-lasting assets—structures and equipment that we would call "capital goods" if they were purchased by businesses. The debts are repaid according to a schedule based on the expected lifetime of the goods purchased. Thus, taxpayers pay for a school, courthouse, sewer system, and so forth, as they enjoy the benefits. Each obligation is being paid back methodically on schedule. This procedure is much fairer than one that puts the entire burden on the taxpayers who happen to live in the area at the time the outlay is made.

The federal government also acquires structures and equipment that last for many years, but makes no distinction in its borrowing between these and other outlays. An aircraft carrier, a federal office building, or a NASA research center is charged entirely to the tax-payers while it is being constructed, even though its benefits will continue for years, maybe decades.

If Washington used financing practices similar to those employed by businesses and by state and local governments, people might rightfully refer to a large part of federal deficit spending as "government investment." Instead, the United States' budget portrays purchases of assets with long lifetimes as expenses of the current year only. Farsightedness is disguised as shortsightedness.

Federal fiscal policy is the only appropriate tool for regulating the flow of profits. Properly used, it will contribute to neither inflation nor government financial instability. On the other hand, monetary policy is not an appropriate tool for maintaining optimum profitability. To see why, we look at the banking system.

A commercial bank is a part of the business sector whose products are financial services. It lends money to companies and individuals, usually for constructive purposes, and provides other services that facilitate transactions and the smooth operation of the economy. Like any firm, a bank competes with rivals for customers and profits. By being innovative and efficient and by making good decisions, it can prosper.

Competition tends to ensure that society has enough banking services, just as it usually ensures sufficient quantities of automobiles, ovens, and pencils. The greater the demand for loans by credit-worthy businesses, the more banks will lend. If nothing interferes with the banking market, the industry will tend to grant loans to any individual or business that is sufficiently likely to meet its obligation. That is exactly what it ought to do.

The banking system is regulated by various government organizations, including the Federal Reserve. Their job is to keep the industry running honestly, soundly, and in a manner that will enable it to meet legitimate demands for credit.

Nowadays the Board of Governors of the Federal Reserve System and many economists, politicians, and business people believe that the central bank should reign over the economy like a god on Olympus. The followers of this faith, monetarists, believe that an economically omnipotent central bank should sometimes adopt measures that limit the ability of banks to extend credit. In effect, government should prevent banks from making loans to qualified companies and individuals who want to increase the production of desired goods and services. The monetarists believe that such measures will strengthen the economy, but they are actually advocating that the Federal Reserve keep the economy from fulfilling its function.

Most monetarists are proponents of free markets, but they want the Federal Reserve to interfere with credit markets. They apparently do not realize the inherent contradiction in their position. Limiting the amount of credit that banks can grant is as clear a case of interference with a market as exists. The government should not interfere with banks' ability to make responsible loans any more than it should restrict the amount of steel that mills can produce. Indeed, if, during a prosperous but inflationary year, Washington ordered all steel producers to limit their output to 85% of last year's tonnage, everyone would know that the government was reducing the size of the economic pie and creating unemployment.

A "tight steel" policy would cause an immediate slump in automobile production. Although its damaging effect on auto sales would be similar to the consequences of a "tight credit" policy, fewer dealers would be driven into bankruptcy; they would have empty lots instead of large inventories of unsold cars financed with bank loans at onerous interest rates.

The supply of steel used for construction, machinery, and household appliances would, of course, be short. Major industries that depend on steel would therefore have to furlough employees, most of whom are well-paid union members. Unemployment would be useful in slowing the upward trend of wage rates. Moreover, because reduced steel output would limit the production of capital goods, lead to a reduction in inventories, and result in less consumer borrowing to buy automobiles, washing machines, and other appliances, the flow from the sources of profits would diminish. Consequently, profit margins would narrow. Advocates of "steel restraint" would hail its success in fighting inflation.

If the government ever did tell the steel industry, "You may only sell 85% as much steel as last year," or "You must double your prices," leaders of industry, union officials, and millions of other Americans would scream for it to leave the economy alone. And they would be right. Yet many of the supporters of free enterprise, who would be among the first to admonish the government for interfering with the steel industry, applaud similar interference with credit markets.

We said earlier that monetary policy can influence a number of the profit sources but should not be used to regulate the flow of profits. The reasons are beginning to become clear. Tampering with the monetary system can prevent the banking industry from doing its job and cause undesirable side effects. But that is not all.

Monetary policy is an unreliable tool for regulating the flow of profits. Suppose the flow were inadequate and the government wanted to use monetary policy to stimulate the credit-sensitive profit sources. The Federal Reserve would take measures that would ease lending restrictions and lower interest rates. But if investors were anxious about the future, if people were hesitant to buy houses, if industry had large excess capacity, a drop in interest rates might not have much of an effect on borrowing or therefore on profits. After all, monetary policy has only an *indirect* effect on profits, unlike the government deficit, which is itself a profit source.

Attempts to lead the economy out of a recession by easing credit restrictions have often been compared to "pushing on a string." This analogy was certainly apt during the Great Depression. Although credit was readily available, and interest rates on commercial loans at major banks were less than 2%, practically nobody wanted to borrow. What good was a loan to build a new factory when less than 50% of the capacity of your existing plant was being utilized? What good was a favorable mortgage rate if you could not afford the down payment on a house?

Although credit and low interest rates may not themselves bring about a recovery, they are nonetheless prerequisites for a return to prosperity. When a stringent monetary policy contributes to an economic slump, credit must be eased in order to enable a recovery to occur. The severe recession that began in 1981 was caused by tight credit and the resulting high interest rates. Moreover, the persistence of high rates hindered recovery.

Monetary policy should not be used to regulate profits. It should not be used to fight inflation. It should be used to assure readily available credit. Markets should set interest rates that reflect lenders' evaluations of their risks, uninfluenced by government-imposed scarcities of money. No credit-worthy firm or individual with legitimate needs for funds should be unable to secure a loan because of "tight money."

The right fiscal and monetary policies will assure an optimum flow of profits and full employment, but they cannot cure our present inflation. Fiscal and monetary measures that cause profits to fall sharply and unemployment to climb toward depression levels can slow or even halt the upward trend of prices, but only until the economy is again moving toward prosperity. Such a respite from inflation is purchased at a high price—severe damage to the economy and widespread, growing doubts about the justness of capitalism. The loss of faith in the system is likely to lead to increased political strength for groups that are not sympathetic to private enterprise.

If we want to fight inflation, we have to face the problem squarely. That is not easy. Rising prices are telling us some things that we do not want to hear.

# 12

## The Inevitable Inflation

*Prices rise when sellers raise them. Why do they raise them? Either to increase their profit margins or to protect margins following an increase in operating costs.* Indeed, the two basic causes of inflation are *rising profit margins* and *increasing business costs.* Profit margins can become excessive when the flow from one or more of the profits sources rises, which can happen for a number of reasons—speculation by business in inventories, ill-advised government deficit spending, a surge in exports, and so forth. Costs can also rise for a number of reasons.

Inflation, then, is the name of a symptom, not a disease. Just as a doctor must determine what disease is causing a fever in order to administer the proper medicine, we must diagnose the causes of inflation before we can prescribe a remedy. The treatments for excessive profit margins and rising costs are not the same.

"Excessive demand," an "overheated economy," and "too many dollars chasing too few goods" are phrases often used to describe inflation. These terms are relevant only when rising margins cause inflation—when an excessive flow of profits enables businesses to charge excessive prices. Excessive profit margins indicate that society is asking its economy to produce more than it currently can. So much profit is being offered to firms as an incentive that the business sector is unable to expand enough to stay competitive. The economy is malfunctioning.

Although profit margins can sometimes make a significant con-

165

tribution to rising prices, they cannot by themselves cause inflation to continue indefinitely. Prices will remain too high as long as margins are excessive; but once margins stop rising, they do not contribute to *further* price increases—at least not directly.

But excessive profit margins tend to "pull" costs up. When the flow of profits is too great, sellers find that they have an unusual number of eager customers. They expand to take advantage of the situation, hiring more workers in the process. As unemployment disappears, the possibilities of achieving still more production become limited. Competition is lax. Companies, urged on by exceptional opportunities for profit, are willing to pay higher wages. As a result, wages and salaries are bid up.

The result is more inflation. Rising employee compensation only inflates prices—and profits—further. Margins, which are unaffected by rising wages, will stay high, and firms will try to hire workers away from one another. The process will continue until something happens to reduce the net flow from the profit sources.

Excessive profits have occurred twice in the United States since World War II, but not in recent years. Profits were too large following the outbreak of the Korean War in 1950, and again after the United States expanded its participation in the Vietnam War in 1965. The average profit margin for the business sector peaked around 1966. It declined gradually until 1969, then dropped more rapidly as the 1969–70 recession developed. During the following 12 years, it seldom reached an optimum level. *Except for a few years in the mid- and late Seventies, when employment was rising smartly, profits have generally been inadequate since 1967.*

Because profit margins have not been excessive, *price instability in the 1970s and early 1980s was not the result of "too many dollars chasing too few goods."* Not enough dollars were "chasing" goods to induce full employment. As we saw in the last chapter, an overabundance of money in the economy cannot bid prices up without raising profit margins. Although margins fluctuated during the years 1969–81, they showed no evidence of "excessive demand." While the amount of money in the economy rose greatly, we will see that it did so as a *consequence* of inflation, not as a cause.

Moreover, since the profit margins of the business sector have been either optimum or less than optimum for over a decade, *the federal deficit has had nothing to do with inflation during this entire period*. This statment is likely to seem incredible in view of contemporary economic erudition, but unless the deficit leads to excessive profit margins, it cannot inflate prices.

If sellers are raising their prices, and their profit margins are not rising, only one diagnosis is possible: costs are rising. *Inflation from 1969 to 1981 was the result of rising business costs.*

Labor is the largest cost of the business sector. It has two determinants: employee compensation rates and worker productivity. When employee compensation rates increase, labor costs increase. When worker productivity increases, business pays less to get a job done. Both rising compensation rates and stagnating productivity in the United States have made critical contributions to inflation.

Until the 1970s, we Americans were living in a world of plenty. Natural resources were abundant. But now we are living in a world of paucity because of burgeoning population and increasing industrialization. From 1960 to 1980, the number of human beings increased from about 3 billion to 4½ billion. As a result, the need for materials to feed both people and industries vastly increased. Such diverse products as oil, herring, and cobalt became more difficult to obtain, and their prices, as well as those of other materials, rose at what were perceived to be excessive rates.

As a result, a substantial proportion of price increases reflected *real costs*—costs measured not in dollars but in hours of work and in the use of plant and equipment. To obtain oil on the North Slope, transport it across Alaska, pump it into ships, and unload it at a port in California costs more than drawing petroleum from a conventional well in Oklahoma. Prices do and should reflect real costs, including, in this instance, the costs of pipelines, tankers, and specialized work crews.

We are not accustomed to an economy in which the real costs of many materials are increasing. We are used to one where real costs declined as a result of technological progress, where the expanding application of scientific knowledge brought us a higher standard of living. By using new labor-saving machinery and improving the efficiency of mines, factories, and other operations, industry was able to bring us more automobiles, household appliances, and other products at increasingly affordable prices.

Now, however, we often need more workers and more machinery than formerly to extract a ton of iron ore or a thousand cubic feet of natural gas from the earth. We frequently incur such increases in real costs when we try to obtain many basic products. This fact of economic life reduces the probability of a rising standard of living. No economic policy can compensate for nature's failure to be infinitely bountiful.

We, and people in other industrialized nations, refuse to believe that real costs of many important products are increasing. When fish, lumber, and fuel oil become more expensive, we reckon that their prices are out of line. We are like a man we heard about some years ago who had Abercrombie & Fitch ship a barometer to his home in Florida. The barometer came back to the distinguished New York store with an angry note complaining that an obviously faulty instrument had been delivered. "Its indicator," the letter said, "was pointing to extremely low pressure in an area of the dial marked 'hurricane.'" The postmark indicated that it had been mailed just before one of the more devastating hurricanes on record had hit Florida. That storm destroyed the home of A&F's erstwhile customer.

Like the Floridian's maligned barometer, price increases caused by rising real costs bear unwelcome—but inexorable—news. Inflation does not reduce the standard of living; rather, it reflects reductions in the standard of living. It tells us, when the prices of goods and services rise beyond our reach, that our real purchasing power is decreasing. *To the extent that prices account for rising real costs, they are doing what they are supposed to do; they are doing their job.*

In 1973, an extraordinary phenomenon was occurring at commodity markets. A great many prices soared. Cocoa, copper, corn, cotton, lead, silver, and other prices took off, often doubling. Demand, it seemed, was everywhere outrunning supply. Then, in 1974, the prices of sugar, petroleum, and other commodities joined the inflationary trend. Oil became the prototype of inflation. The world's growing population of trucks, buses, and passenger automobiles and the increasing industrial and agricultural use of petroleum brought customers in ever greater numbers to the countries that have oil to export. Inexorably prices rose.

Unprecedented prices led geologists to search for what would formerly have been highly uneconomic deposits of petroleum. Meanwhile, engineers began figuring out how to get oil from shale and how to make liquid fuels from coal. The gas and gasoline that will eventually come from oil shale and other novel sources will cost a great deal more in man-hours and equipment than the fuels we have been accustomed to obtaining.

Oil is an outstanding but not a peculiar situation. Another example of the lengths and expense that firms go to in their quest for materials is a mile-and-a-half-deep silver mine in Arizona. At other locations, silver comes from mines that were once abandoned because the remaining ore was deemed too poor to exploit. Extracting silver from these mines or extremely deep ones is much more expensive in real terms than obtaining the metal from the rich, relatively shallow lodes, which in many cases have been exhausted.

Minnesota's Mesabi range was once the source of excellent iron ore. The rich ore was exhausted, and now the area supplies taconite, from which iron-ore pellets are obtained with considerable effort and at great cost. A few years ago, that cost was increased by the necessity of building and operating expensive facilities to forestall the pollution of Lake Superior. This story is going to be repeated again and again for other materials.

Scarcities of fish are already apparent. Fishermen often need larger boats than they used a few decades ago in order to travel farther and stay at sea longer. Nations try to preserve finite resources for their own exploitation by limiting the access of foreign boats to the fishing grounds they control. Because of these restrictions, international incidents have occurred in U.S., Peruvian, Icelandic, and other waters where fishermen from a number of nations vie for the available catches. Rapidly diminishing populations of some varieties of fish have led countries to cooperate to protect the disappearing species.

The world now produces enough food to nourish its population, partly because of the considerable improvements in farming methods that have recently been achieved in many developing areas. Where starvation and malnutrition do occur—in such places as Kampuchea and Bangladesh—a grotesque political program or extreme poverty is responsible, not a global dearth of fertile acreage. But Earth's supply of food may not keep pace with its growing population. Farmlands in the United States and elsewhere are being overrun by burgeoning cities and suburbs. Soil erosion and desertification claim tens of thousands of acres annually. Meanwhile, each year brings an additional 75 million stomachs worldwide that need food.

Greatly increased world harvests are possible. They will require the use of modern methods in countries that are still relying on their traditional farming practices. Fresh advances in agricultural science are also needed. If the world's food production does not increase at least 25% from 1980 to 2000, future food prices may make OPEC at the height of its glory look like a collegium of pikers.

Higher real costs occur not only when materials are difficult to reach but also when we buy a number of products from other countries. For example, at the beginning of the Seventies, the United States traded an Oldsmobile or its equivalent for 10,000 pounds of coffee from South America. A decade later, South Americans demanded two Oldsmobiles for 10,000 pounds of coffee. We had to devote at least twice as much manpower and use at least twice as much of our plant and equipment in order to exchange our products for many of those we imported—for lead, coffee, silver, tin, and other items. Worst of all, America's real costs for imported petroleum rose fivefold in less than a decade. Our real—as distinguished from dollar—costs of many imported items have been increasing over the long term and will continue to do so.

These worsening terms of trade have been adversely affecting the U.S. standard of living since 1973. The unfavorable trend is revealed by a comparison between *gross national product* and our indicator, *gross available product*. GNP measures the goods and services that our economy produces; GAP accounts for the goods and services that are available in our country for domestic use. The goods and services that the United States produces for export are part of its gross national product. These exports are not available for use or consumption at home. The goods and services that this country imports do not increase GNP, but they do increase our available goods. Thus:

Gross national product (GNP) = domestic product kept at home +domestic product exported

Gross available product (GAP) = domestic product kept at home +foreign product imported

Figure 18 shows that from 1965 until 1974, the growth of both

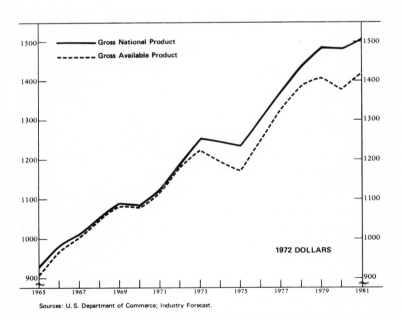

Sources: U.S. Department of Commerce; Industry Forecast.

Figure 18. Gross National Product and Gross Available Product

GNP and GAP, measured in 1972 dollars, was about the same. But since then, GNP, our output of goods and services, has grown faster than GAP, our available goods and services. Because of steeply rising prices of oil and other materials, we have had to export much more of our gross national product than formerly in order to obtain the same quantity of imports.

Although sometimes GAP will rise faster than GNP, the longer-range prospect is that Americans will have to work harder in order to import the same materials. However, should world grain prices surge because of global food scarcities, the United States will be able to trade wheat, corn, rice, and soybeans on highly favorable terms.

Technology has a new task in the world of scarcity. In the past when an industry replaced its old equipment with new machinery, it almost invariably lowered its costs. But now a goal of many industries is to obtain materials, even if they can be acquired only at increased cost. Investments in plant and equipment do not always result in higher productivity; they occasionally result in less productivity.

For example, engineering advances will make important contributions to the world's supply of petroleum for some decades to come by exploiting deposits beneath the oceans. But they do not promise cheap oil. Offshore oil-production platforms that are designed to withstand heavy seas may cost $250 million each. In the 1970s, these structures operated in waters no more than 800 feet deep. In the 1980s, they will draw oil from wells in much deeper waters—undoubtedly at higher costs.

Another example of new technology being used in high-cost operations is a facility planned by the Homestake Mining Company in California to obtain gold. Sometime in the 1980s, Homestake expects to be mining particles of the precious metal so small that they cannot be seen with the naked eye. Millions of cubic yards of ore, which will yield tiny quantities of gold per ton, will be processed by enormous earthmoving machines. This gold will not be cheap.

That America has to devote more of its manpower and equipment than formerly to obtaining numerous materials is not the sole reason for the recent lack of success in increasing productivity. Output per person-hour has been adversely affected by the trend to a service economy, by regulations needed to protect the health of workers and the environment, and by monetary policy. Changing characteristics of American business have also been a poor influence on productivity.

A serious impediment to gains in productivity has been the strong growth in consumer demand for services, relative to the demand for manufactured products, during the last three decades. In 1950, services accounted for 33% of consumer purchases; by 1980, this figure had grown to 47%. More and more of our expenditures are for services, which by and large do not lend themselves to mass-production techniques. Doctors cannot perform three appendectomies in the same time that they performed one a generation ago. Waiters cannot properly serve more people now than they did 30 years ago. Barbers cannot cut hair faster than formerly. Thus, the increasing preference for services has been slowing productivity gains.

As consumers spend more of their incomes on services, their purchasing power becomes less affected by productivity gains in manufacturing. Data published by the Department of Labor on productivity ("output per hour of all persons") reveal that the most significant gains in worker efficiency occur in manufacturing. From 1970 to 1980, output per hour of all persons for the entire business sector rose an average of 1.4% annually. In manufacturing industries alone, the average increase was 2.5%—not impressive by international or historic domestic standards, but considerably better than in the economy at large. Meanwhile, productivity in service industries (for which the Department of Labor does not publish consolidated data) certainly rose much less than in the rest of the economy.

The phenomenal rise of women's participation in the labor force is responsible for much of the nation's growing demand for services. Households with two incomes are likely to spend proportionately more for services than those with one breadwinner. Traditionally the income of a male head of a household purchased the refrigerator, washing machine, and other basic appliances that were present in almost every American dwelling. These products are mass-produced; advances in technology result in their being manufactured more efficiently, and their prices have consequently been considerably less inflationary than those of most other items. But a second important household income rarely buys a second refrigerator, range, or washing machine. It is far more likely to be used to pay for meals in restaurants, dental care, a college education, and vacation trips.

Because of the ways we consumers choose to spend our money, we are, to a degree, responsible for whatever is disappointing about the productivity of American business. If we spend more of our money for services, we must accept the consequences that our spending decisions have on our economy's productivity, and therefore on the growth of our purchasing power.

A far more important impediment to increasing American productivity has been the misplaced priorities of business.

"When the United States government passes new automobile safety or environmental-protection regulations, the Japanese car manufacturers rush right out and hire more engineers. The American auto producers rush right out and hire more lawyers."

This quip, which has been repeated at cocktail parties and business meetings, may be a little unfair to Detroit. Nevertheless, it does identify a shifting emphasis in many American companies away from production and toward legal and financial concerns.

As an industry matures, the characteristics of its leadership often change. Numerous firms are started by scientists and engineers who want to sell their brainchildren to society. After the new companies are well established, they tend to come under the control of financiers and lawyers, sometimes as a result of mergers. Eventually the scientists move, retire, or fade into the background. Too frequently, the new leadership concentrates on making money through shrewd financial dealings rather than through product innovation and improvements in methods. The highest salaries are used to attract financial talent, not production managers, engineers, and research scientists. Growth means buying additional businesses, not starting them.

An increasingly execrable monetary policy contributed considerably to the diversion of business's efforts from finding ways to increase productivity and improve products to discovering means of advantageously shuffling existing assets. In the latter 1960s and in the 1970s, experiments with tight money contributed to a generally rising trend of interest rates. Many billions of dollars that ordinarily would have bought common stocks were used to purchase Treasury bills, certificates of deposit, and other short-term, interest-bearing investments that were offering record rates of return. The consequent lack of support for stock prices helped greatly to depress the stock prices of many companies to levels that were extremely low by historical standards. Corporations could buy stocks of many existing firms—and their factories, machinery, and established markets—at far less cost than they could purchase new plant and equipment and develop new businesses. Under the circumstances, the acquisition of one company by another became a common occurrence. Because they changed the behavior of investors and managements, tight money policies bear some of the responsibility for the failure of American industry to match the gains in productivity that were attained in other industrial nations.

Another phenomenon that is adversely affecting the productivity of American industry is its growing emphasis on short-term profits and consequent neglect of long-term growth. Japanese businessmen shake their heads in amazement at the preoccupation of their American counterparts with next quarter's income statement. The emphasis of American companies on the short-term stems in part from the attitudes of important shareholders who, increasingly, are financial institutions. Today, more than a third of the stock of American companies is owned by pension funds, insurance companies, mutual funds, and other institutions. These investments are in the charge of professional money managers whose reputations, salaries, and jobs depend on whether the stocks in their portfolios go up and to what degree. These managers therefore keep their eyes on the profits of the corporations whose stocks their institutions own as closely as Hank Aaron watched a pitched ball. If a company's latest quarterly report reveals less profit than was expected, the stock is likely to be sold quickly and its price to tumble.

To have a high-priced stock is greatly to the advantage of a corporation because it helps the company to raise new capital on favorable terms. So the firm's executives try to maximize profits quarter by quarter—often by not spending much money on the equipment and research that would enhance the company's long-range prospects.

The common prescription to achieve good gains in productivity is to buy more new factories and machinery. Business leaders, economists, and politicians generally believe that tax incentives encourage capital investment. In the postwar United States, these inducements have been the tax advantages provided by the investment credit and faster rates of depreciation. These incentives were sweetened by many of the tax laws adopted between 1950 and 1981.

Yet a tax break seldom persuades business to invest in new machinery. Industry buys equipment for other and better reasons. Usually executives know whether or not new equipment will be worth its cost. Only on the few occasions when the issue is in doubt will the investment credit or a fast write-off tip the scales in favor of going ahead.

Tax incentives rarely induce business to make investments in new facilities when a large proportion of its existing plant is idle. But when times are prosperous, almost every company will want to expand and modernize to meet rising demand. If a firm fails to do so, it will lose customers to competitors who are aggressively taking steps to reduce costs and increase sales by purchasing new plant and equipment.

While special tax inducements to promote capital investment may not be much help, government-imposed impediments to new construction are probably a significant hindrance. The legal obstacles and the red tape that sprang from legislation aimed at limiting pollution have undoubtedly impeded investment in new structures. No longer does a company buy a piece of land, design a structure, arrange for its financing, and build. It has to demonstrate that the building will be ecologically virtuous. To some degree, these circumstances will be with us for the foreseeable future.

Protecting the environment slows the acquisition of some equipment but it also leads to investments in machinery that would not otherwise have been made. Devices that are necessary and desirable in order to prevent factories and vehicles from polluting are often installed only because the law demands them. Investments made to prevent the fouling of the environment usually reduce output per person-hour, but in the long run the financial and other benefits from cleaner air and water are likely to outweigh the short-term losses in productivity.

A far more serious hindrance to capital expenditures than anti-pollution laws and other government regulations has been the policies of the Federal Reserve in recent years. Although chairmen of the central bank have been prominent in deploring what they see as inadequate investment, the Federal Reserve has periodically raised the cost of new money beyond the reach of many companies that need it in order to purchase new plant and equipment.

The prime requisite for a healthy rate of capital outlays is that the central bank does its job—makes sure that an ample supply of credit is available to take care of the needs of business. The worst aspect of the Federal Reserve's activities that adversely affect capital investment is their impairment of the flow of vital funds to small businesses. Budding companies are the ones that make most of the important innovations that lead to greater efficiency and therefore downward pressures on prices. Eastman Kodak did not develop the photocopying process that led to a huge new industry. An unknown little company that later changed its name to Xerox did. Long-established companies were not the creators of minicomputers; nor did many of the major makers of semiconductors, the elements that make modern computers possible, exist two decades ago.

Typically, a small company that is fortunate enough to have the genius to create a new and highly useful product needs large infusions of capital as it moves along the path to success. During a period of tight credit and high interest rates, it may not be able to borrow at rates it can afford and it may have difficulty in raising equity capital. Grave damage has been done to the productivity of American industry by the periodic scarcities of credit that business has endured since 1966. No one knows how many tender young companies with promising products were snuffed out by the Federal Reserve's tight credit policies or how many others had their growth seriously impeded by its misguided anti-inflation tactics.

During any period, tight money or any other government economic policy that interferes with the production of goods and services is reprehensible. Such ill-conceived policies are especially pernicious in these times of growing populations and scarce resources.

The increasing difficulty of meeting world demand for many mineral and agricultural products marks the end of an era that commenced with the birth of the Industrial Revolution. No economic policy can restore, at least in this century, the world of seemingly unlimited resources. Nor can any humane program reduce the number of Earth's inhabitants and the need for materials to run their expanding industries. Indeed, the growth of world population requires the use of more machinery to feed and otherwise provide for humanity. Food-producing industries must nourish 40% more people than they fed two decades ago. Because of industrialization, the demand for most materials has increased more than 50% during the past 20 years.

As long as increasingly greater efforts are needed to obtain many materials, their prices will rise. Because these materials are used to make many other products, their prices, too, will rise. The function of prices is to reflect such real costs. Thus, some inflation is inevitable in the 1980s.

But most of the inflation Americans have been experiencing in recent years is not inevitable. It is unnecessary.

# 13

## The Unnecessary Inflation

Recent American inflation has been, to a considerable extent, an index of our dissatisfaction with our standard of living. A variety of phenomena, including the rising real costs of many materials, have tended to reduce our real purchasing power. The response has been dismay, frustration, anger, and efforts by individuals to obtain more money. Workers have fought for and obtained wage increases as if higher pay rates could somehow produce more goods. Unfortunately, what the higher wages produce is still higher prices.

During the 1970s, almost all American workers, from janitors to corporate executives, competed for pay increases in the contest called "catch up with inflation." Most of them played the game well and continually won large raises. In so doing, they accelerated the rate of price advances. *Indeed, rising labor costs—the result of employee compensation increasing faster than productivity—was the major inflationary force of the 1970s.*

As illustrated by events in A-land and B-land, wage rates do not rise at the expense of profits. When employee compensation increases, inflating labor costs, profits rise, too. The result is higher prices with no improvement in the nation's standard of living. If some workers gain purchasing power, other workers—or people living on savings—must lose it. Because rising wages cause approximately proportionate increases in the economy's flow of profits, firms have generally been able to grant pay increases, raise their prices, and maintain their profit margins. In the 1970s, as 7%, 8%,

179

and even larger wage raises became commonplace, companies routinely increased their prices to cover the higher costs.

The only way to offset the inflationary influence of pay increases on labor costs is to improve productivity. Unfortunately, the United States has been notably unsuccessful in this respect. From 1973 to 1979, when wages were rising at the rate of approximately 8% annually, productivity increased at the rate of only 0.9% a year. By contrast, in West Germany, where wages were increasing about 7% annually, productivity gains were five times as great as in the United States. The resulting difference in labor costs was the principal reason why Germany's consumer prices advanced about half as fast as America's.

Great Britain, like the United States, has had large pay increases in recent years without significant gains in productivity. The British experience from the middle 1970s to 1980 is a particularly dramatic demonstration of rising wages acting as an inflationary pressure. In 1974 and 1975, unions in the United Kingdom were often achieving 30% annual raises, and consumer prices were at times increasing faster than 30% a year. Meanwhile, the economy was faltering in other respects, including profitability. No one doubted that less inflation would have to be preceded by smaller wage increases. The government adopted measures that reduced average raises by almost two-thirds. As a result of this program, British inflation slowed to an average rate of less than 8% for the year and a half ending December 1978.

But labor grew restive with wage restraints and, more fundamentally, with the stagnant or declining standard of living. Strikes, which often caused considerable damage to the economy and annoyed many people, became commonplace. Employers, including, at times, the government, overlooked the official restraints on pay increases. The upward trend of wages accelerated.

In May 1979, the Conservative government came into power and adopted a program of fiscal and monetary restraint that was practically irrelevant in the face of rising pay rates. Before mid-1980, the trend of wages was upward at a rate of about 20% annually. Prices were rising somewhat faster. Not until the government's program

considerably curtailed economic activity did the trend of wages—
and with it, the trend of prices—rise less sharply.

American inflation in the past decade has not been as virulent as
its British counterpart, but it has just as surely been fueled by pay
increases. Figure 19 illustrates the close relationship between in-

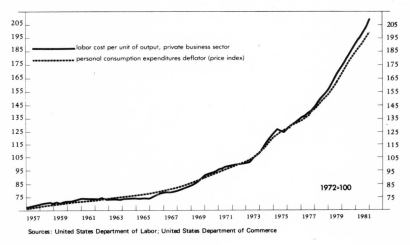

Figure 19. Inflation and Labor Costs

creases in labor costs and rises in prices. It also explains why employees who achieved raises did not enjoy increases in purchasing
power for long. Their plight was reminiscent of Tantalus, whose
thirst was never quenched in Hades because the waters receded every time he leaned forward to drink.

Clearly, stabilizing the average compensation rate in any economy beset with soaring wages and salaries will eliminate a major
source of inflation. But the forces behind pay increases are deeply
rooted and powerful. They reflect ingrained attitudes, overblown
expectations of rising purchasing power, misconceptions about how
the economy works, and the failure to accept its limitations. Recessions suppress these inflationary forces—1982 was an outstanding
example—but prosperity releases them. These forces derive a great
deal of their strength from dissatisfaction with the standard of living.

Several extraordinary occurrences curtailed the growth of the

American standard of living in the 1970s. Productivity—which had risen ever since the Depression, bringing ever-greater consumer purchasing power—plateaued. Higher real costs for petroleum and other materials contributed to the stagnation of productivity, and also adversely influenced our terms of international trade, reducing our gross available product. Meanwhile, an unprecedented demographic phenomenon had a further negative effect on the average size of a slice of economic pie. Greater longevity and the proliferation of pension plans caused the population of retirees to burgeon. These people were consumers, but they no longer made substantial contributions to production. They consumed a growing proportion of the pie produced by active workers, reducing the size of everyone's share.

The American standard of living would have fared even worse during the 1970s had it not been for another unusual demographic development—a record increase in the size of the labor force—which somewhat mitigated the explosion of the retired population. Two independent phenomena were responsible for the great increase in the number of workers helping to produce the pie. First, most of the 41 million people born during the baby boom of the 1950s became adults and went to work during this period. Second, and even more dramatic, women began seeking and obtaining jobs in both business and government in unprecedented numbers. Women who had raised their children entered the labor force; women leaving school sought careers; even women with young children managed to juggle their schedules to include both household and job responsibilities. Between 1970 and 1980, the growth of the population was responsible for about 6 million females joining the labor force. Sociological changes, which encouraged women to seek employment, brought an additional 8 million women to the nation's offices, factories, and other places of work. The change of our economy from one in which most women were not employed to one in which women generally hold jobs will soon be largely completed.

Because of the approaching stabilization of female participation in the labor force and the declining number of births after 1959, the labor force will grow much less rapidly in the 1980s than during the middle and latter 1970s. Thus, the number of producers of the economic pie will be increasing less rapidly. Meanwhile, productivity will, at best, crawl upward. For these reasons, the pie will expand slowly.

But the number of consumers will continue to grow rapidly because of increasing longevity. While the total population expanded 11% from 1970 to 1980, the number of persons aged 65 and over increased 27%. The number of retirees grew 50%. The growth in the number of elderly people will continue to be disproportionately high in the 1980s. Already there is one retired worker for every four active ones sitting at the table sharing the economic pie. The ratio of retired to active workers will increase in the Eighties. Since the number of consumers may grow faster than the pie, the likelihood is that the slices will become smaller.

An increase during the Seventies in unemployment added 3 million to the number of people who were entitled to a share of the economic pie without producing any of it. From 1975 to 1981, even when the economy was not in a recession, at least 6 million were jobless. At the end of the 1960s, the unemployed numbered about 3 million.

Anyone who has savings or income from wages, pensions, social insurance, or from any source has a claim to a share of the economic pie. In 1980, over 30 million workers who were not employed, either because they were retired or had been laid off, had a claim to pieces of the pie. Their number, largely because of the expansion of the retired population, will keep growing rapidly.

Although the prospects for a significantly better standard of living in the near future are not cheerful, the appetites of all those workers, retirees, and other consumers are as insatiable as ever. We have been indoctrinated by sophisticated salespersons who work in both the government and business sectors to believe that standards of living ought to be noticeably higher than they are. As a result, we delude ourselves; we believe that we can have more goods and services than we create.

Our problem begins with the ways in which most Americans measure their standard of living. When government sends space shuttles into orbit, compels industry to pollute less, supports cancer research, bolsters the nation's defense, or revitalizes the local sewage system, the typical American does not feel that his economic well-being is improved, even if he favors these actions. He counts only such things as TV sets, automobiles, the number of rooms in his dwelling, trips to the movies, kitchen appliances, vacations, clothing, and the quantity and quality of meat on his table.

Americans should realize that their standard of living measures not only their own personal purchasing power but also goods and services the government buys on their behalf. The economic pie comprises national defense, criminal justice, and education as well as TVs and lamb chops. Obviously there is a trade-off between the amount of purchasing power individual consumers retain and the amount they give to government. They cannot have more police protection without giving up something else unless the pie becomes larger. Ultimately, the public pays for the goods and services it receives.

Politicians are largely responsible for deluding Americans by diverting attention from this trade-off. Public support for many government services has been won by selling tactics that would, if employed by private corporations, be questioned by the Federal Trade Commission, the Securities and Exchange Commission, or some other official policemen. Governments always have new or additional benefits to sell, although the catalog changes with the political winds. Sometimes the service is medical care for the aged and indigent; on other occasions, it is military power to resist communism. In either instance, the government is selling survival, a popular item. The salespersons seldom, if ever, tell taxpayers how much it will cost them individually, if indeed they are told that it will cost anything.

Not only the urgings of politicians but also the advice of our society at large have created unrealistic economic expectations. Traditionally, Americans have believed that the road to wealth is paved with college textbooks. Undeniably, education does enhance many individuals' abilities to contribute to the economic pie. Moreover, the benefits of higher education to individuals and society go well beyond the marketable skills that come from college courses. But society has led many of us to believe that schooling has greater economic importance than in fact it does. Half of the nation's high-school graduates enroll in colleges. Many of them assume that they will attain positions of importance with high salaries. Yet no more than 20% of the jobs in our economy require a person to have a college education, and we could probably get along fine if only 10% of the population had baccalaureates. Thus, our society implicitly makes grand economic promises to its students that, in many cases, cannot be fulfilled.

Although higher education's economic promises to individuals are often exaggerated, its benefits to society are not. Education prepares people to be discerning consumers, productive workers, informed voters, and useful citizens in other respects. But it is not a sure ticket to affluence.

Our educational system and government are not the only institutions that contribute to breeding disappointment with the standard of living. Business is in some ways the worst villain when it comes to creating an exaggerated belief among consumers of what their standard of living ought to be. Through commercial TV, it creates an immeasurable amount of dissatisfaction with our standard of living. When commercials are directed to children, this issue is one of considerable notoriety. Anyone who has dealt with the insistent requests made by kindergartners who have been watching TV commercials selling cereal or toys has some idea of the power of the medium.

Adults presumably have more sales resistance than children, yet they may easily be victims of TV's broader economic message: "You should have *more!*" If archeologists in the year 6982 discover some TV station's library of videotapes and view the commercials, they will certainly have a favorable impression of the American standard of living 5000 years earlier. Watching one television advertisement after another reinforces a vision of affluence well beyond the reach of the American family with average income.

The dissatisfaction television creates among the nation's poor must be particularly great. In 1980, one out of four families had pretax income of under $12,000 a year. These people do not have much discretionary purchasing power for movies, theater, spectator sports, and so forth. As a result, they find a great deal of their entertainment on TV. They watch television for many hours a week—often 45 or more, according to surveys. An impression of the world and of a "normal" standard is being thrust on them that cannot increase the satisfaction they feel with their lot in life. Television contributes to the notion that they are somehow being shortchanged by the economy. The commercials they watch that show a kitchen or a backyard or some other aspect of a home invariably portray one with appointments that the typical family, let alone a poor one, cannot afford.

The median family income, before taxes, was about $22,000 in 1980. Obviously, many of those who sell the wares advertised on TV are interested primarily in families whose incomes are above the median. And as one advertising executive explained, "We sell dreams." The family with $22,000 is encouraged to have $35,000 dreams.

The programmers as well as the advertisers sell dreams. Stories on the video tube are likely to be about people who live in rather luxurious homes, drive late-model automobiles, work in beautiful offices, drink and eat in good restaurants, and often travel by airplane. Seldom are TV programs about families who live on $12,000 or less. When television turns to nonfiction, it still creates the impression that most of its viewers have a less than acceptable standard of living. The young woman who helps present the morning news works in a well-appointed studio. Her clothes are not from J. C. Penney but from Saks Fifth Avenue. None of her male colleagues are tailored by Montgomery Ward. And all of them visit their hair stylists regularly.

Business and government continually present us with a lovely image of how we ought to be living. No one tells us how to be satisfied with the standard of living that we can attain. The consequences are worry, unhappiness, and unrest. To know how widespread this distress is, one merely has to listen to our countrymen. Despite the nation's high standard of living, people complain about their struggle to purchase what they regard as necessities. Many of them have been impelled to saddle themselves with debt to a greater extent than ever before in order to maintain the standard of living that they believe they should have. For even a quite affluent family that sends one or more children to college, this economic stress is a difficult and serious matter.

Most people have blamed inflation for their dissatisfaction. "Because of inflation," many have said, "I had to cut back on my purchases." Actually *Americans cut back on their purchases because the population of consumers was growing faster than production.* These cutbacks would have occurred with or without inflation.

Nevertheless, most Americans refuse to accept the reality that our standard of living is no longer rising. When prices soar, they blame inflation. When recession dampens the price trend but creates unemployment, they blame the poor state of the economy. They continue to feel unjustly deprived of purchasing power, and they vent their frustration by pulling out all stops to obtain higher pay whenever economic conditions will permit. As long as the economy is not in a recession, most employees are able to win substantial raises year after year.

Although some rising prices are inevitable, the major cause of inflation—rising employee compensation—is not. We Americans, despite our reputation for being pragmatists, have been living in a fantasy world. We are so involved with trying to grab bigger slices of the economic pie that we are unable to see that the pie has not been growing as fast as the number of consumers. We have grandiose visions of the economy's ability to provide us with goods and services. For these reasons, we fail to understand that rising compensations do not increase the average portion of pie, but they do fuel inflation. *Most of our inflation is unnecessary.*

Limiting wage and salary increases is not an easy task. Rising compensations reflect deep-seated attitudes and unrealistic expectations. To teach Americans that they cannot consume more than they produce is an uphill struggle, especially when politicians, labor leaders, and business often suggest the opposite.

Until now, the remedies prescribed to cure inflation have dealt largely with symptoms. These prescriptions are not effective against the powerful underlying forces that have been responsible for rising prices. They counteract neither the effects of increasing world demand for materials nor our unrealistic expectations of a rising standard of living.

But these remedies do have an effect. They cause trouble.

# 14

# Bad Medicine

In October 1979, with the tacit approval of the president and the Congress, the Federal Reserve adopted a program of increasing unemployment, reducing corporate profits, widening the federal deficit, restraining productivity, and lowering the standard of living. The policy was credit restraint. The government's objective was to strengthen the American economy. One may well wonder what more effective actions could have been taken if the goal had been to weaken the economy.

This program, designed to assure stable prosperity by bringing inflation under control, was founded on erudite nonsense. Nothing like it has dominated the beliefs of humankind since Ptolemy taught that Earth is the center of the universe and that the other celestial bodies in our solar system revolve around it. The Ptolemaic system was based on the observation that the sun appears in the East at dawn, moves across the sky, disappears in the West, and again appears in the East the following morning, Clearly, the sun must circle the earth!

Policies of monetary restraint are based on the observation that the money supply moves with or ahead of prices. The conclusion is that the way to get rid of inflation is to hold the money supply down. Tragically, this belief, unlike Ptolemy's theory, is a cause of widespread misery.

Monetary policy must assure ample credit to meet the legitimate requirements of borrowers, or else injure the economy, perhaps seriously. It is an extremely crude anti-inflation weapon. To slow rising prices even temporarily, it must damage the economy.

Nonetheless, as a result of misunderstandings about the economic realities of the times, many capitalist countries are fighting inflation with tight money. This perilous strategy has caused high unemployment and recessions. The prospects for restoring prosperity while applying the monetary remedy for inflation are bleak.

Monetarists exaggerate the role of money in the economic system. They claim that the performance of the economy is almost entirely dependent on money. They are preoccupied with the amount of money in the system and the institutions that create it, but they pay little attention to the reasons why it is created. They overlook the relationship between credit and the flow of profits from its sources.

Thus, monetarists blame the growth of the money supply for inflation while ignoring the actual causes of rising prices. They pay little attention to the rising demand for and depletion of the world's resources and to the resulting increases in real costs. They are indifferent to the negative influence of these rising costs on the standard of living. They are not concerned with the reactions of workers who are dissatisfied with their purchasing power. Monetarists take the narrow view that inflation is simply the result of the money supply growing too rapidly. The way to stop it, in their view, is to prevent rapid monetary growth.

Monetary policy cannot prevent real costs from rising. It cannot replace the oil in an empty well or put iron ore back in an exhausted mine. Nor does monetary policy have much to do with a worker's degree of satisfaction with his standard of living. It cannot turn a plate of spaghetti into filet mignon, or a transistor radio into a stereo system. It cannot explain to an employed worker that a rapidly growing population of retirees is leaving him a smaller portion of the economic pie.

Historical data on the growth of the money supply show that the amount of money in our economy tends to grow faster during periods of inflation. This observation has led many people to conclude that a growing money supply *causes* inflation. They err. Inflation causes increases in the money supply.

How can this be?

Suppose company A raises wages. In order to maintain its profits, it must pass its increased costs along to its customer, company B. Company B then has to borrow more money from its bank in order to purchase higher-priced materials from company A. If company B cannot obtain more credit, it will be unable to carry on its usual activities. It will then have to reduce production and furlough some of its employees.

Rising labor costs for company A and many other employers are inflationary. These cost increases lead to demands for more credit. If the banking system does not create this credit, it causes a reduction in business activity, even a recession.

Thus, government finds itself in a dilemma if it is using monetary policy to control inflation. The government must either prevent rapid monetary growth and cause the economy to slow, thereby risking a recession, or it must repeatedly loosen the central bank's restrictions on credit, and allow the economy to keep moving forward. Since the U.S. government until 1981 had sought to avoid recessions, and to bring any recession that occurred to a rapid end, it had no choice but to periodically ease monetary policy.

Changes in the money supply should be regarded as a gauge of inflation, not an instrument for adjusting it. To try to control inflation by holding the money supply down is like trying to keep an automobile engine from overheating by tampering with the temperature gauge on the dashboard—only worse.

Since monetary policy can influence neither real costs nor workers' satisfaction with their purchasing power, how does it fight inflation? By squeezing profit margins and by creating unemployment. Tight money curtails the flow of profits into the business sector. Competition among firms becomes too intense, forcing many to reduce prices and cut back their operations. As business contracts, unemployment becomes widespread and pay rates rise more slowly.

The deflationary effect of narrowing margins is often substantial, although it can last for only a short time. During a typical recession, shrinking margins tend to reduce prices by 2%–3% in a period of about six months—that is, they would cause an annual rate of deflation of about 5% if labor and other business costs did not change.

For example, if business costs were rising at an annual rate of 8%, causing 8% inflation, and the profit margins narrowed at an annual rate of 5%, the inflation rate would temporarily drop to 3%.

In a recession, moderate declines in profit margins experienced in turn by raw-material suppliers, manufacturers, wholesalers, and finally retailers aggregate; they result in considerable price reductions for the ultimate customers. But the inflation-fighting benefits last only as long as margins keep narrowing. When they stabilize, as they eventually must, they no longer reduce prices. Moreover, once the economy begins to recover, margins start to widen, giving inflation an extra boost. The 2–3% is added back to prices—on top of whatever other inflation is occurring as a result of rising costs.

*Only by causing a serious recession with a high rate of unemployment can monetary policy sustain its deflationary influence.* As profits tumble and jobs disappear, many of the workers who remain employed become increasingly aware of the financial difficulties of their employers. These employees worry that they, too, may be discharged. Their bargaining positions weaken and they accept smaller pay increases than formerly. As a result, labor costs rise at a slower pace, and inflation eases. The counterinflationary effect of unemployment continues throughout the recession. However, the economy's resistance to inflationary pay increases dissipates once a recovery is under way. As the rolls of the unemployed decrease, workers' bargaining power gradually returns. Employees obtain increasingly large raises. Business passes the higher labor costs along to consumers.

Thus, when tight money is used to fight inflation, "monetary policy" is really "unemployment policy." The strategy pursued by the Federal Reserve after October 1979 was not advertised as a plan to break the trend toward higher pay by putting many workers out of their jobs, but only by creating unemployment could it have any effect. Meanwhile, few people in the United Kingdom had any doubt that the monetary policy adopted by their new Conservative government was designed to fight inflation with unemployment. Between 1980 and 1981, credit restraint boosted the jobless rate from 5% to 12%. The unemployment policy worked—to a degree. The rate of pay increases fell from over 20% annually to less than 10%.

Many Britons would argue that their government had to adopt an unemployment policy in order to contend with a unique problem, one that had relatively little effect on the economies of other industrialized nations. The output per worker in the United Kingdom has been about half as much as in the United States, West Germany, France, and some other advanced countries because of union work rules and long-established customs that interfere with output. Some drastic economic trauma, the defenders of the unemployment policy would contend, was needed to convince workers that they must relinquish their counterproductive privileges. And, indeed, the unemployment policy *has* succeeded in bringing about gains in manufacturing productivity. Whether these improvements will stick at such time as Britain returns to high-level employment remains to be seen.

The unemployment policy was adopted in the United States by the Federal Reserve in October 1979, only months after it was inaugurated in Britain. Advocates of this policy maintain that the credit reins must be pulled with vigor and persistence—in effect, that monetary control must be used to create enough unemployment, an adequate number of bankruptcies, and a long enough lull in the economy's efforts to become more efficient through investments in modern plant and equipment.

That tight credit has been purposefully used to bring about all of these unhappy conditions is not contested. Here is what Lyle E. Gramley, a member of the Board of Governors of the Federal Reserve System, said in March 1981:

> When monetary restraint takes hold, it reduces employment and real incomes; pushes interest rates to painfully high levels, threatens the viability of thrift institutions, imposes enormous loss of sales and profits on homebuilders, auto dealers, and other small business, results in a growing backlog of needs for housing, and even affects adversely the growth of business capital investment that we so badly need for productivity improvement. And its effects on inflation occur with agonizing slowness.

Mr. Gramley's statement is both eloquent and accurate. Yet it makes us wonder what our country is coming to. Mr. Gramley's words were spoken in *support* of the Federal Reserve's tight credit policy.

That the unemployment policy works with "agonizing slowness" is a post–World War II development. A period of rising unemployment, no matter what its cause, has always served as a medicine for treating inflation. But in the latter half of the twentieth century, this medicine has been losing its effectiveness. Prior to World War II, recessions and their concomitant unemployment caused wages to decline. Since then, recessions have lost much of their counterinflationary potency. Increased union bargaining power, scarcities of specialized workers, and the high costs of training new employees have interfered with the market mechanisms that once made recessions deflationary. Longer-term labor-management contracts and cost-of-living adjustment clauses have further reduced the effectiveness of economic contractions as anti-inflation weapons. Therefore, *recent business slumps have only slowed the rate of pay increases.* From 1970 to 1980, the wage-and-salary rate trend was barely affected by periods of rising unemployment.

The record is revealing. Wage rates were 8% higher in 1948 than in 1947. Then came the 1948–49 recession. In 1950, wages rose only 3.7%. Thus, the recession led to a drastic (more than 50%) attenuation of a basic inflationary force. The average pay increase in 1953 was 5.7%. Then came the recession of 1953–54. In 1955, wages rose 3.2%. Again, a crucial decline in a basic upward pressure on prices. The next peak in annual wage increases was 5.2% in 1956. In the aftermath of the 1957–58 recession, wages rose only 3.4% a year. The recession of 1960–61 occurred after a relatively brief interval. In its wake, wage increases came down to 2.7%. That was the end of an era in which the downward phases of the business cycle engendered significant anti-inflationary forces.

The annual wage rise in 1969, the eve of the 1969–70 recession, was 6.6%. By 1972, wages were increasing even faster, 7% a year. The advance did slow—to 6.4% in 1973 and 6.2% in 1974. From 1975 through 1981, the annual wage increases ranged between 7.3% and 8.3%.

Clearly the 1969–70 recession and the severe drop of 1974–75 failed to cut wage increases drastically. And no real relaxation of wage increases occurred as a result of the brief 1980 recession. But the severe slump that began in 1981, before the economy had fully recovered from the 1980 contraction, caused a considerable decrease in the rate of pay raises early in 1982.

No quick cure of inflation can be achieved through monetary policy. Tight money can be successful in slowing the trend of rising prices only after a long and painful period of abusing the economy. Nevertheless, tight money became the keystone of our government's anti-inflation campaign. The successive recessions that began in 1980 and 1981 were entirely the result of monetary "medicine."

Slowing the economy enough eventually leads to a substantial reduction in the rate of inflation. The relaxation of upward price pressures in early 1982 is an excellent example. The rate of inflation was cut by more than half because of rapidly narrowing profit margins and a considerably reduced rate of pay increases. But the inevitable problem of restoring prosperity without reviving inflationary measures remained. Advocates of the unemployment policy have no solution to this problem.

As long as government relies on the central bank to fight inflation, the outlook is not cheerful. What we can look forward to, if no change in emphasis is forthcoming, is an indefinite period in which the rate of unemployment will be high, productivity will be impeded, and no lasting gains against inflation will be achieved.

Monetary policy is not, of course, the only instrument for implementing the unemployment strategy of fighting inflation. Fiscal policy can be used to assure an inadequate flow of profits just as effectively as it can contribute to an optimum flow. The effect of unemployment on the economy and on inflation is essentially the same whether it is caused by fiscal or monetary measures. The primary difference is that the use of fiscal policy to create unemployment does not distort credit markets. It does not interfere with the system's ability to properly allocate to firms whatever profits flow into the business sector. Still, too small a deficit or too large a surplus causes widespread misery, inadequate investment, bankruptcies, and other woes.

Like the banking system, the federal government's fiscal policy has a specific job to do. Its job is not fighting inflation—that is, not unless inflation is being fueled by generally excessive profit margins. Fiscal policy should make sure that an optimum amount of profits flows into the economy. It is not a proper instrument for fighting the kind of inflation caused by rising costs of work and basic materials—the kind of inflation that is likely to be a chronic problem in the remainder of the twentieth century.

Monetary and fiscal policy are the most widely recognized ways of treating an economy that is suffering from inflation, but not the only ways. Unfortunately, most of the alternative and supplementary prescriptions also fail to address our underlying difficulties.

One of these prescriptions is to encourage consumers to save. Its advocates say that more saving is necessary to increase investment and therefore productivity. Unfortunately, increasing consumer saving, while our economy is in its present state, would be highly undesirable. Investment would not be encouraged; it would tend to decline. The proponents of increased saving err in their reasoning.

The notion that more saving will mean more investment comes from the axiom, saving = investment. Indeed, if saving increases, so will investment. Thus, if consumers save more, the argument goes, businesses will invest more in efficient plant and equipment, and American productivity will rise.

The flaw in this logic is that saving is not just personal saving but the sum of personal, government, and business saving. Business saving includes undistributed profits. Increases in personal saving, a negative profit source, will reduce the nation's flow of profits. Therefore, business saving will decrease and offset the increase in personal saving. Total saving will not rise. Meanwhile, firms will have less incentive to invest, so investment will decline, and profits will decline further.

*To accommodate additional investment, personal saving need not rise.* When businesses are motivated to invest, business saving will automatically rise to maintain the balance between total saving and investment.

Another prescription for curing inflation is price controls. This traditional remedy has not been tried in the United States since 1972. The concept is so simple that it appeals to many people. They hold that if the law says prices cannot rise, and the law is enforced, prices cannot rise.

The reasoning behind price controls may be direct, but it is simplistic. When prices are frozen, markets cannot operate properly. The consequence of price controls would be especially troublesome in these times when real costs are often rising. What would happen to controls if OPEC raised its prices or the cost of mining copper rose above its ceiling price? Even during wartime, when real costs were relatively stable and people had great patriotic incentives to adhere to controls, the programs worked imperfectly. The result of price controls in the 1980s would be shortages of many products, black markets, and, before long, the complete disintegration of the controls program.

Still another prescription, indexing, is not intended as a cure for inflation but as a means for coexisting with it. Indexing has become familiar to more and more Americans in recent years as cost-of-living adjustments "indexed" to the rate of inflation have been written into a growing number of labor contracts and pension plans. Some people would like indexing to become much more widespread in order to cover all wages, salaries, debts, sales contracts, and so forth. If we cannot keep prices from rising, they reason, let's at least allow everyone to keep up with inflation.

Countries that have tried this plan have found that it merely greases the wheels of inflation and makes prices rise so fast that money loses almost all meaning. Indexes cannot create a larger economic pie. In fact, the time and effort that governments, businesses, individuals, and their accountants and lawyers spend trying to make sure that everything is properly indexed increases costs and reduces the size of the pie.

None of the popular remedies for inflation are going to give us a healthy economy with full employment and stable prices. The reason: none of them requires that the American people face the facts of life in the late twentieth century. None of them copes with the rising costs that are consequences of the physical limitations of our planet and the dissatisfaction of our workers. Such remedies cannot work.

Even under ill-advised policies, inflation will sometimes ease, giving the impression that the malady is being cured. Were the government to do nothing about rising prices, inflation would moderate at times and intensify at others because business costs do not increase at a steady pace. For example, in some years the prices of major crops decline as a result of huge harvests even though their long-term trends are flat or upward. Surpluses of oil and other materials occur every now and then as reactions to previous large price increases. Prices of these commodities fall for a while, but after a number of months, a year, or two years, they again move higher. Worker productivity, which has an important effect on prices, also varies from one year to the next. All these phenomena can reduce inflation in the short run.

Should enough of these deflationary developments coincide, inflation would be greatly alleviated for the moment. Whatever Washington might be doing at the time would be regarded by many as a cure for rising prices. But a year or so later, they would be looking for a new remedy.

If we seek a miracle cure for our current economic malaise, one that will restore 1960s-type gains in our standard of living, we are bound to be disappointed. Growing world population and industrialization mean a rising demand for natural resources. Under the circumstances, industry and agriculture often have to go farther, dig deeper, and exploit poorer resources in order to provide us with their products. Real costs rise. No economic drug can change this reality.

Whenever reasonably prosperous conditions prevail in our highly specialized economy, labor markets cannot prevent wages and salaries from rising—so long as pay demands are fueled by powerful sociological forces. As long as workers feel victimized, dollar labor costs will rise. None of the cures discussed in this chapter can improve people's satisfaction with their standard of living.

America's economic interests lie in making every reasonable effort to put as many people to work as possible. We can use as much economic pie as we can produce. Unemployment policies intended to improve the health of our economy are intolerable.

As long as programs aimed at reducing inflation slow the economy without addressing the fundamental causes of our soaring prices, the future will be grim. Little or no lasting progress will be made toward restoring price stability; growth in output and gains in productivity will be stunted; and all the while, millions of people will endure unnecessary hardship.

But the economic fate of the United States is not sealed.

# 15

## America's Opportunity

The United States *can* enjoy prosperity—full employment; a relatively low rate of inflation; profitable, expanding business; and confidence in the stability of its economy. Even though we Americans may have to abandon expectations of a significantly higher standard of living in the immediate future, the average portion of our economic pie could be getting noticeably larger by the early 1990s.

America has bright opportunities. Whether we take advantage of them remains to be seen. If the United States continues monetary policies that limit growth, it will perpetuate unemployment, inflation, an unnecessarily low standard of living, and economic uncertainty. If our government adopts even more restrictive credit policies than those that were in effect in the early 1980s, conditions will become even worse.

Dismay over our disappointing economy, over chronic unemployment, continuing inflation, a stagnant standard of living, and declining ability to compete against other nations will engender feelings of anger and frustration. The American people, desperate to find a way out of their economic troubles, may grasp at nostrums recommended by politicians who are pressured to "do something." The confused climate may jeopardize the political and economic freedoms of American society.

Alternatively, we can realistically face the challenges before us and take constructive steps to revitalize our economy. These measures would greatly increase the output of desired goods and services, and, for all practical purposes, eliminate unemployment. We can assure prosperity.

We Americans have been living in a world of make believe, imagining that the average individual's purchasing power should grow continually. Yet the United States' standard of living has of late been static or declining. This divergence between fact and fancy has led most of us to think that someone, somehow, has been cheating us. We put the blame on OPEC, unions, multinational corporations, former presidents—any person or place that enables us to avoid facing basic realities. We do not care to recognize that our economic pie has been growing more slowly than our population of consumers.

Full employment is not only a goal but also a means for achieving a higher standard of living and combating rising real costs. Naturally, the economy can produce more when more people are at work. Furthermore, productivity tends to grow faster over the long term when the economy is at full employment than when many workers and capital goods are idle. The reason is that full employment encourages investments in labor-saving plant and equipment. It does this in three ways.

First, full employment necessarily coincides with a sufficient flow of profits into the business sector. When jobs are plentiful, firms generally enjoy comfortable profit margins and experience high rates of utilization of their plant and equipment. Nothing motivates business to invest in new capital goods as much as satisfactory profits and a lack of idle capacity. Almost inevitably, the new plant and equipment are more efficient than older facilities.

Second, full employment puts pressure on many employers to invest in labor-saving capital goods. When unemployment is high, managers have relatively little trouble finding additional workers to expand their output. It is often easier to add a few people to the payroll than to investigate more productive options, purchase new equipment, and implement new procedures. However, when qualified job applicants are difficult to find, businesses are much more aggressive about investing in capital goods that will increase the productivity of their present employees.

Third, when jobs are readily available, workers are less resistant to the introduction of labor-saving equipment than when employment opportunities are scarce. New machinery and other facilities are often perceived by employees to be threats to their jobs—usually with good reason. Therefore, they sometimes strongly oppose the implementation of advanced technology, even to the extent of sabotaging the new equipment. Under full employment, workers are less anxious about losing their jobs because other positions are open. Moreover, when business is profitable, companies that replace workers with machines are likely to have other needs for the displaced employees. Workers will be redeployed, not released.

In a full-employment economy, innovations that increase productivity—even those that make jobs obsolete—are in the best interests of the working class. We saw in chapter 11 that technological progress does not reduce the aggregate number of jobs in the economy, but it does raise the nation's standard of living. It also increases the desirability of many jobs.

This last assertion may seem surprising in view of traditional ideas. Ever since the days of Adam Smith, mechanization has been criticized for dehumanizing workers by transforming craftsmen into automatons. But today, labor-saving innovations often liberate workers from highly repetitive, tedious tasks. The automaton may once again be a thinking human being with more responsibility and more interesting work. He may direct and maintain industrial robots that tirelessly and precisely perform his old job. A typist becomes a word processor; a clerk learns to use a computer terminal; a stock-room hand operates a mechanized inventory-retrieval system. Throughout the economy, new technology is making jobs more pleasant and more responsible.

Full employment will occur if government ensures an optimum flow of profits. It is an elusive goal only because unemployment, according to the prevailing erudition, is necessary to fight inflation. Had the Federal Reserve allowed the banking industry to adequately service the economy in 1980–82, profits, investment in plant and equipment, and employment would have moved ahead briskly. Another benefit would have been a reduction in government deficit spending. A monetary policy that supplied adequate amounts of credit would have quickly caused a vast increase in the Treasury's tax receipts, a result of higher corporate and individual income. Meanwhile, its payments of interest on the national debt and such outlays as unemployment-insurance benefits and aid to families with dependent children would have decreased.

Instead, our economy is ailing. It has a disease that has produced the symptom of inflation, but it is also suffering from bad medicine that in the long run aggravates the symptom. The doctors attending to the economy ought to adopt a strategy of fighting the disease, not the patient.

The disease is excessive pay raises. As long as wages and salaries rise substantially faster than worker productivity, inflation will persist. *To be effective, any anti-inflation policy must somehow restrain raises in wages and salaries during prosperous times.*

The medicine generally prescribed to fight inflation is one form or another of the "unemployment policy." So far, it has had only moderate, temporary effects on the rate of pay increases. In addition to all the other damage this remedy has done to the economy, it has had some disturbing effects that promise to aggravate inflation in the long run. By discouraging investments in new plant and equipment that would increase worker productivity, the unemployment policy has promoted higher business costs for years to come. *Any constructive anti-inflation policy must not interfere with efforts to increase productivity.*

Wages *can* be restrained. In some of the world's most successful economies, government, business, and labor have cooperated to prevent excessive pay increases. Perhaps the United States may achieve similar success in limiting this major source of inflation in the years ahead. We can take heart from the results of wage-restraint policies in other nations.

One of the countries that has limited pay increases is Japan. When a Japanese company negotiates with workers, both parties resolve to reach an agreement that fairly rewards employees without jeopardizing the company's competitive position. Government encourages business and labor to keep wage and salary increases moderate. Generally, there is a consensus that compensation should not rise faster than productivity. As a result, little of Japan's inflation is the result of increasing labor costs. The inevitably rising real costs of imported materials, from fuel to food, are the primary cause of increases in Japanese prices.

Can the United States match Japan's success at restraining pay increases? The differences between the two nations may raise doubts about our ability to achieve the necessary consensus. While Japan is a homogeneous society with an Oriental culture that emphasizes group rather than individual identity, we are a diverse collection of individualists.

Yet another country, one with a culture similar to our own, has been remarkably successful at keeping a lid on pay raises. Austria is much smaller than the United States, and its people, like the Japanese, are quite homogeneous. But life in Austria—as represented by such diverse elements as food, religion, the arts, and even eating utensils—resembles life in the United States.

Austria's gross national product grew faster in the 1970s than that of any other Western European country, except Norway. (Norway's GNP was given a substantial boost by its newly tapped North Sea oil reserves.) Austrian inflation was among the mildest in the world, averaging only 5.3% from 1975 to 1980, compared to 8.9% for the United States. American inflation grew worse as the Seventies progressed, but Austrian inflation was lower in the second half of the decade than in the first. While the U.S. unemployment policy was limiting jobs, not prices, only 2% of the Austrian labor force was unemployed.

Austria's secret is essentially the same as Japan's. In the land of mountains, Mozart, and strudel, business, labor, and government reach a consensus about appropriate pay raises just like their counterparts who eat sushi half a world away. Everyone agrees that full employment must not be jeopardized, and that to control inflation pay raises must not outstrip gains in productivity. Austrian unions have realized that higher pay increases would only lead to more inflation. *They have accepted the necessity of small pay increases even on occasions when rising costs of imported raw materials have offset gains in productivity and reduced the standard of living.*

The Austrian sense of national purpose and cooperation is a source of strength that enables that country to fight inflation constructively. Its government does not resort to tactics that damage the economy.

One of the other countries that reached consensuses on noninflationary wage increases was the United States. From 1959 until 1966, the prevailing belief among businessmen, union leaders, economists—indeed the general public—was that wages should increase 3% annually because productivity was rising at about that rate. Americans observed this standard with little, if any, prodding by government. During this period, hourly wages rose at the average annual rate of 3.1%, and the United States experienced less inflation than at any other time in the post–World War II era. Meanwhile, America's standard of living grew at a steady pace. People were generally pleased with the performance of the economy.

But two decades later, times had changed. By the early 1980s, Americans had been experiencing difficulties in maintaining their purchasing power. Many people felt that they somehow were being cheated. Workers placed increasing emphasis on the need to "catch up with inflation" regardless of the size of the raises required to achieve this objective.

The unsatisfactory conditions of the 1970s led to policies that were at cross-purposes with one another and with the objectives of our economy. Americans lacked the Japanese and Austrian understanding of what needed to be done to reduce inflation while promoting the growth of the standard of living.

Americans should be able to rely on their government for an explanation of the nation's economic situation. Government in a democratic society ought to inform the public about any threat to the country's welfare, be it military, natural, or economic. Unfortunately, the government has repeatedly misinformed the American people. Political leaders representing almost every point of view have been contributing to Americans' unrealistic expectations by making promises that the economy cannot fulfill. For example, many advocated tight money without disclosing its long-term costs

in terms of unemployment and lost investments in plant and equipment. Candidates of all parties have told Americans to be satisfied
with nothing less than rising real purchasing power. Yet few politicians have done any homework on the standard of living.

Surprisingly enough, almost no one forecasts the standard of living on an ongoing basis. You will have a hard time finding the term
"standard of living" in the more than 200 pages of any recent issue
of the *Economic Report of the President/Annual Report of the Council of Economic Advisers.*

Government can make a constructive contribution to the public's
understanding of what realistically to expect from the economy by
regularly issuing forecasts of the standard of living. As experienced
economic forecasters, we maintain that this job can be accomplished reasonably well with the data and knowledge now generally
available and understood.

A forecast of the standard of living by the president's Council of
Economic Advisers would alert the press and political leaders to the
likely purchasing-power problems of the American people in the
periods ahead. When the outlook was poor, newspapers and broad-
casters would have a big story. The media would report that Americans should expect a lower standard of living. People who listen to
the usual political promises and are mesmerized by the dreamy
world of TV would have a chance to become acquainted with reality.

The premise of our democracy is that most of the people will
face reality at least some of the time. Reality is that we have to pay
higher costs for many materials. Reality is that our population of
consumers is growing faster than our population of workers. Reality
is that our standard of living may not grow in the 1980s.

If we Americans are going to make significant strides against unnecessary inflation, we must accept basic facts of economic life that
the Japanese and Austrians already understand. First, we must recognize that we cannot consume more economic pie than our economy
produces, and that the average slice may sometimes shrink. We
must be ready to bear that disappointment without rushing out and
demanding excessive pay increases. Even if inflation came to a dead
stop and every worker had a job, discontent would prevail as long as

people felt that they were being deprived of purchasing power. Such discontent would impel them to seek higher compensations. Until Americans become realistic about the standard of living that the economy can provide, they will not support constructive efforts to limit inflation by restraining rates of compensation.

At times, workers have expressed, somewhat reluctantly, a willingness to accept restraints on pay raises, but only on condition that corresponding limitations be imposed on income from profits. This point of view is based on the notion that if only wages are held down, profits will rise and purchasing power will thereby be shifted from workers to investors. Thus, the Marxist myth stands in the way of Americans accepting restraints on pay raises.

American workers and investors must realize that they have common rather than conflicting economic interests. A raise does not change the size of the portion of the economic pie that goes to investors. Wage increases merely redistribute pie among workers, and between workers and those living on savings or fixed incomes. A function of wages is to distribute the employees' share of goods and services equitably.

But even if Americans generally accept the need to limit pay increases, we cannot expect that one day wages will spontaneously stop rising at inflationary rates. Someone has to provide leadership. That someone is obviously the government. Elected officials in Washington must set forth a program for limiting pay increases. Employers and employees need a standard to adhere to when negotiating wages and salaries.

We hope that Americans will understand the problems of the economy, particularly inflation, and will respond in the way that the Japanese and Austrians have. But most people in our country have not faced reality, the prerequisite for effectively and constructively dealing with inflation. Before progress can be made, attitudes must change.

If Americans will not accept pay restraints, the alternatives are not cheerful. Two developments are possible: one is a secular trend of worse inflation; the other is a continually sluggish economy with high unemployment, poor productivity, unsatisfactory standards of living, and chronic recessions.

With no restraints on inflation at all, the familiar spiral of pay increases, price increases, and more pay increases to catch up with inflation will continue. Although the rate of price advances will fluctuate, the long-term trend will be increasingly virulent inflation. In such an economy, financial markets cannot function properly, consumers find it difficult to save, and wealth is constantly and un-justly redistributed.

On the other hand, as long as tight money or some other form of unemployment policy continues, the economy will not run at a reasonably high rate of capacity. Whenever the flow of profits is approaching an optimum rate, and business is therefore becoming eager to invest in new plant and equipment, employment, too, will be rising. The bargaining power of workers will be increasing. Wage raises will become larger. More inflation will result. Then the un-employment policy will be used to slow activity once again.

Under these circumstances—which would prevent the American economy from using all its resources—the standard of living, indus-try's ability to meet foreign competition, and faith in the system would all suffer. More of the countries that pursue policies to main-tain optimum profitability and full employment would move ahead of the United States in per-capita gross national product and stan-dard of living.

If the American people know the causes of inflation, have realis-tic expectations, and understand the options, they will be in a posi-tion to decide which means of controlling inflation is preferable. We predict that they will choose to limit inflation by restraining increases in compensation. After all, Americans are pragmatists.

The problems the United States faces in the 1980s are not nearly as serious as those that it encountered in the 1930s and 1940s. We have neither intractable depression with 20% unemployment nor a world war. The difficulty of increasing the average standard of living in the Eighties should not be regarded as onerous by Americans who have at least average incomes. Conserving expensive heating fuels, driving smaller automobiles than formerly, and substituting chicken for steak are mild sacrifices, not serious deprivations. The unemployed and other less fortunate Americans should be able to look forward to an improvement in their economic status. Our present is far from disastrous, and our future may indeed be prosperous.

Although coping with "the world of scarcity" may become still more challenging in the 1990s, the outlook for the standard of living is encouraging—if the United States adopts constructive economic policies. The demographic trends that are impeding the growth of our standard of living in the 1980s will not be a hindrance in the following decade. The population of retirees and other nonworking consumers will grow much more slowly in the 1990s than at present. The number of Americans 65 years of age and older will increase by 5 million from 1980 to 1990, but by only 2 million during the final decade of the twentieth century. Whereas the ratio of active workers to retirees is decreasing in the Eighties, it will rise during the Nineties.

Before the end of the century, burgeoning advances in technology may significantly improve our standard of living. Already, companies are entering a new industry, biotechnology, which may eventually revolutionize medicine and agriculture and help increase the availability of energy. Meanwhile, the still young electronics industry is continually making advances that will lead to major increases in productivity. We see dramatic demonstrations of this trend when robots substitute for human beings on factory assembly lines and when electronic tellers who are on duty 24 hours every day facilitate bank deposits, withdrawals, and other transactions. All the sciences—including biology, chemistry, and physics—are designing a more comfortable, affluent world for us.

The building blocks for a bright future are here. Only a poorly functioning economy will prevent us from putting them to good use. We need to understand our economic system and operate it properly. Then we can adapt to a world of limited resources, assure prosperity, and achieve a stable economy.

# Notes on Methods Used
# in Chapter 5

These notes outline the major estimates and simplifications in the analysis in Chapter 5 and discuss their effects on the sources of profits of the consumer- and capital-goods sectors. As indicated below, none of these simplifications affect our end result, the list of profit sources for the entire business sector.

### *Splitting the Business Sector*

The division of the business sector is our own creation. The Department of Commerce does not provide statistics for each sector separately. Therefore, we estimated what portion of wages, net foreign investment, changes in inventories, and capital consumption allowances should be attributed to each sector. Since these were all either totaled or canceled out in the course of our analysis, the final result—the sources of profits for the entire business sector—is unaffected by our estimates.

### *Interest Expenses*

We ignored this business expense entirely when we calculated the profits of both the consumer-goods sector and the capital-goods sector. However, the net effect of these payments on profits is like the effect of wages: zero.

Interest payments by one firm to another do not concern us because they are intrasector transactions. (By definition, any business that loans money to another must be in the same sector.)

Interest paid to consumers is compensation for services, just as wages are. The only difference is that interest is paid for the services of people's money instead of the services of their minds and bodies. The pipeline diagrams for these flows of money would have been identical to those for wages except for the labels and dollar amounts. The consumer-goods sector's interest payments to the household sector, like its wages, have no effect on its profits; and the capital-goods sector's interest payments to the household sector, like *its* wages, add to the consumer-goods sector's profits and reduce its own profits. The net effect on profits is zero. Because of our omission, the equations for the sources of profits for each of the two subsectors are simplified and thus not quite complete.

Finally, interest payments from either sector to the government affect profits in the same way as nonincome taxes and fees paid to the government, discussed below.

## Nonincome Taxes and Fees Paid to Government

Any payments of taxes or fees that are business expenses go to the government sector. When the government spends these funds, they become consumer-goods-sector revenue. Thus, the taxes and fees paid by the consumer-goods sector have no effect on profits; those paid by the capital-goods sector reduce its profits and add to consumer-goods-sector profits. Again, the net effect on profits is zero. And again, we see that the equations for the two subsectors are not quite complete.

## Dividends Paid to State and Local Governments

A small fraction of dividends is paid to state and local government pension funds. Our tally of profits correctly takes them into consideration.

# Index